Appliqué
for
MODERN
Beginners

Eva Birch
Nancy Gano
Jodi Robinson

American Quilter's Society
www.AmericanQuilter.com

The American Quilter's Society or AQS is dedicated to quilting excellence. AQS promotes the triumphs of today's quilter, while remaining dedicated to the quilting tradition. We believe in the promotion of this art and craft through AQS Publishing and AQS QuiltWeek®.

CONTENT EDITOR: CAITLIN RIDINGS
GRAPHIC DESIGN: ELAINE WILSON
COVER DESIGN: SARAH BOZONE
PHOTOGRAPHY: CHARLES R. LYNCH
ASSISTANT EDITOR: ADRIANA FITCH
DIRECTOR OF PUBLICATIONS: KIMBERLY HOLLAND TETREV

Additional copies of this book may be ordered from the American Quilter's Society, PO Box 3290, Paducah, KY 42002-3290, or online at www. ShopAQS.com.

Attention Photocopying Service: Please note the following—Publisher and author give permission to print pages 28–29, 35, 43, 49, 56, 63, 70, 77, 84, and 91.

American Quilter's Society

www.AmericanQuilter.com

Library of Congress Cataloging-in-Publication Data

Names: Birch, Eva, author. | Gano, Nancy, author. | Robinson, Jodi, author.
Title: Appliqué for modern beginners / by Eva Birch, Nancy Gano & Jodi Robinson.
Description: Paducah, KY : American Quilter's Society, [2016] | Includes bibliographical references.
Identifiers: LCCN 2016024937 (print) | LCCN 2016026773 (ebook) | ISBN 9781683390053 (pbk.) | ISBN 9781683395065 (E-book)
Subjects: LCSH: Appliqué--Patterns. | Quilting--Patterns.
Classification: LCC TT779 .B64527 2016 (print) | LCC TT779 (ebook) | DDC 746.44/5--dc23
LC record available at https://lccn.loc.gov/2016024937

COVER: CONFIGURATION, full quilt, p. 30.
TITLE PAGE: AT THE CABIN, full quilt, p. 20.
RIGHT: WHAT A TWEET BABY!, full quilt, p. 85.

Acknowledgments

I want to thank our "foremothers" for their creativity and hard work. They truly paved the way for us today. I am thankful for all the talented individuals out there making our jobs so much easier with the development of our tools of the trade. Being a traditional, scrappy, utilitarian quilt junkie, I am so enlightened and inspired by the modern quilt movement. I can now say I am addicted to modern quilts! Special thanks to my good friends, Linda Roberto for your help with the finishing touches and Lori Walters for the not so "quilty" but tremendous emotional support to see this dream become a reality.

Nancy

I want to thank my fellow co-authors and friends Nancy and Eva. Working with the two of you on this book kept the whole process FUN! It was my pleasure to work with you guys and see our dream of this book become reality. Thanks to my husband, Gary, for his support, and his willingness to eat a lot of frozen pizzas while I worked away on my book quilts. Thanks also to my son, Josh, for his creative support as I second guessed some of my design choices.

Jodi

I would like to thank Jodi and Nancy. Our friendship has become a stepping stone to many adventures that have led us to co-author this book. We make a great team! I can't wait to see what comes next! I especially want to thank my husband, Tim, for always encouraging me to believe in myself and for supporting me, no matter what. Thanks for being my biggest fan!

Eva

Thanks to Kimberly Tetrev, Ginny Borgia, and the entire staff at AQS for giving us the opportunity to share our passion!

Many personal thanks to our dear friend Gayla Pittman. She is our biggest cheerleader, our coffee maker, our color advisor, our design assistant, our encouragement, and our late night full of laughs, good hearted Gayla!

Contents

6 Introduction

8 Supplies

11 Appliqué Methods

16 Finishing the Quilt

19 Projects

    20 AT THE CABIN

    30 CONFIGURATION

    36 INTERCHANGE

    44 METRO

    50 MODERN PETALS

    57 PATHWAY

    64 RUN-OFF

    71 SLICE IT UP

    78 URBAN GARDEN

    85 WHAT A TWEET BABY!

93 References and Resources

94 About the Authors

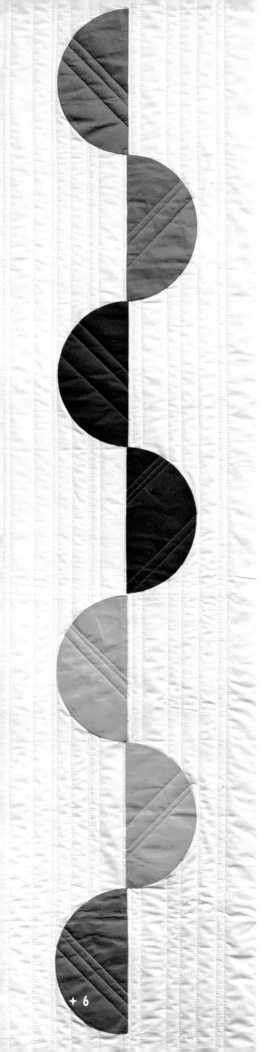

... Introduction ...

The goal of our book is to show you how making Appliqué Quilts can be manageable as well as enjoyable. We have designed each of the quilts using minimal piecing, large scale appliqué shapes, and bold color choices. The results are modern appliqué quilts that can be completed quickly, and provide amazing graphic impact! We have provided step by step instructions for the appliqué methods we used in creating these quilts. If you have a favorite appliqué method you prefer to use, it can easily be applied to complete all of the projects as well. Many of the quilts included in this book are constructed in large sections or blocks, which makes the appliqué process easier and more manageable. If you would like to appliqué by machine, you will not have to wrestle the entire quilt at the machine. The quilts can be worked on in smaller sections, which are then assembled. If you prefer to appliqué by hand, having these individual blocks/sections makes your project portable, allowing you to stitch on the go.

We hope that making these quilts will inspire you, and that you will enjoy the appliqué process as much as we do. Appliqué really can be fun, and the design possibilities it offers are endless!

... Supplies ...

Turned-edge Appliqué

Supplies Needed:

Wash away Stabilizer/Interfacing

The brands we have used include:

    Sharon Schamber – Sharon's Secret Foundation

    Ricky Tims – Ricky Tims' Stable Stuff Poly®

    C&T Publishing – Wash-Away Appliqué Roll

    See resources on p. 93 for purchasing information.

Template Plastic – available at most sewing/quilt shops

Fine Point Sharpie®

Pencil – not mechanical as it can tear the stabilizer

Sharp scissors with narrow tip for trimming

Paper scissors for cutting out the template

Fabric scissors for trimming fabric

Washable glue sticks – there are many brands available, our preference is Elmer's® Washable Disappearing Purple School Glue, it allows you to see which area is glued and it dries clear

Travel Iron – using a smaller iron makes turning the smaller seam allowances much easier

Monofilament Thread – for machine appliqué

Hand sewing needles – for hand appliqué

Raw-edge Fusible Appliqué

Supplies Needed:

Light-weight Paper Backed Fusible Web

The brand we have used is Pellon® 805 Wonder-Under® paper-backed fusible web

Transfer Web – see resources on p. 93 for purchasing information.

Template Plastic – available at most sewing/quilt shops

Fine Point Sharpie®

Pencil – not mechanical as it can tear the fusible web paper

Sharp scissors with narrow tip for trimming

Paper scissors for cutting out the template

Fabric scissors for trimming fabric

Travel Iron – using a smaller iron makes turning the smaller seam allowances much easier

Monofilament Thread – for machine appliqué

Hand sewing needles – for hand appliqué

Appliqué Methods

Turned-edge Appliqué

The turned-edge appliqué method we used to create the quilts in this book is a variation of Sharon Schamber's technique, which is done using wash-away appliqué interfacing/stabilizer. There are many different brands of interfacing/stabilizer available; you will find those that we have used listed in the supply section. To create the appliqué, you will turn the edges around the stabilizer using a water soluble glue stick, and then sew around the edges of your pieces with a small zigzag stitch by machine using invisible thread, or by hand. After the quilt is complete, there is no need to remove the stabilizer, as after the quilt has been washed, the interfacing will partially dissolve and turn into a soft layer of fiber.

Below are the basic steps for creating turned-edge appliqué.

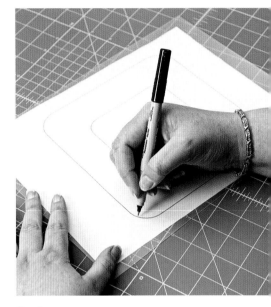

Fig. 1

Create a Template

The first thing you need to do is create a template for your appliqué shape. You will need a piece of template plastic that you can see through, a fine Sharpie® marker, and the shape that you want to use. Simply place the drawing of the appliqué shape under the template plastic and trace with the Sharpie® marker, fig. 1. Using a sharp pair of scissors cut the shape out on the marked lines, fig. 2. Be sure to use a pair of paper scissors to cut the template plastic, as this will dull your fabric scissors. You want to go slow, and cut nice smooth lines, as any bobbles will be transferred when creating the stabilizer shapes.

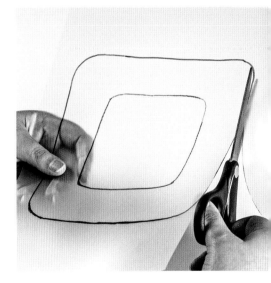

Fig. 2

Fig. 3

Fig. 4

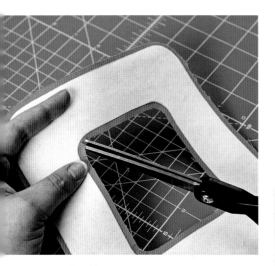

Fig. 5

Make Stabilizer Shapes

Using your template, and a pencil place your template on the stabilizer and lightly trace the number of shapes needed, fig. 3. Be sure to double check the pattern to be aware if you need to reverse the orientation of any of your shapes. Cut out the shapes on the line, being very careful to keep nice smooth lines as you cut, because any bobbles on the stabilizer edges will transfer to the turned edge of your appliqué.

Glue Stabilizer Shapes to Fabric

Place your stabilizer shapes on a piece of scrap paper (to protect your ironing surface) and using a washable glue stick apply glue to the interfacing shapes. You want to be sure to get around all of the edges, and lightly on the body of the shape (be aware that the glue does dry fairly quickly). Place the glued pieces onto wrong side of the appliqué fabric, and press with a dry iron to dry the glue, fig. 4.

> NOTE: It is very important that you use a dry iron throughout this entire process because the stabilizer is water soluble, if steam is used, it can cause your shapes to become gummy.

Trim Excess Fabric

Using sharp fabric scissors, trim excess fabric around the appliqué ⅛" – ¼" from the stabilizer. After trimming, be sure to clip any inside curves up to the interfacing being sure to stay a few threads away from the edge of the interfacing to make it easier to turn under the edges as you go, fig. 5.

> TIP
> Another option when trimming is to use pinking shears. This can be especially helpful when trimming outside curves and circles, as it eliminates a lot of the fabric bulk.

Turned Appliqué Edges

There are a couple of important things to know before you begin the process of turning the appliqué edges. The glue dries fairly quickly so only do one edge at a time. You want to work in small sections, gluing, turning, and pressing as you go. Don't be worried if you find you have an area where your turned edge isn't as smooth as you'd like. Simply pull up a glued area and redo it. The process of turning may seem a little tedious at first, but once you get the feel for it, it will go quickly. Working in small sections, use your washable glue stick to apply glue to the edge of the appliqué foundation, turn the fabric edge, fig. 6, and iron for a few seconds to dry the glue, fig. 7. There are many ways to turn the edges. You may find it easier to hold the shape, and pinch the edges in as you go, or perhaps you prefer to have it on a flat surface as you work, and fold the edges over. Between the three of us, we each do the actual turning portion differently. Our suggestion would be to try a couple of small practice shapes to see what works best for you. This is a great way to get a feel for the process before you start quilting.

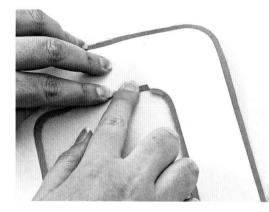

Fig. 6

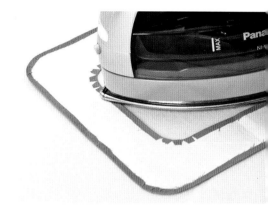

Fig. 7

Centering and Gluing Appliqués to the Background

The easiest way to center an appliqué shape accurately on the background block is to fold, and lightly press your block in half both vertically and horizontally, fig. 8. If you have a shape that is placed on a point in the background block, simply press in half diagonally twice. You will then finger press your appliqué shape in half twice as well. You now have registration points to use for accurate alignment of your appliqué piece on the background, fig. 9, p.14.

After aligning your block placement, you are now ready to glue and attach your appliqué piece to the background. Using your washable glue stick, apply glue to the edges, and body of the shape, fig. 10, p.14, align on the background, and press, fig. 11, p.14. You are now ready to sew your appliqué pieces in place.

Fig. 8

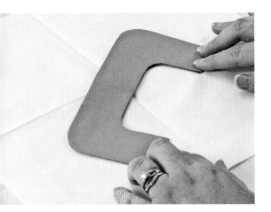

Fig. 9

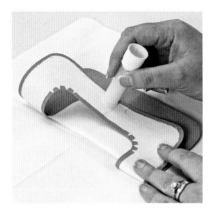

Fig. 10

Fig. 11

Fig. 12

Fig. 13

Stitch Appliqué Pieces by Machine

To sew your appliqué pieces to the background by machine, set your machine up for a narrow zigzag stitch, fig. 12. Thread your machine with monofilament thread in the top and fine cotton or polyester thread in the bobbin. If you have an open toe foot for your sewing machine, it can be very helpful to give you a better view of the needle as you stitch. You want to use the smallest zigzag that you are comfortable using. You want one of the zigzag stiches to land just off the edge of the appliqué piece on the background fabric, and the other on the appliqué piece. We would suggest doing a couple of practice shapes to get a feel for stitching. Experiment with the size of your zigzag stitching to find what will work best for you. For the quilts in this book, we have used monofilament thread which makes the stitching almost invisible, but you can use any type and color of thread you prefer.

Stitch Appliqué Pieces by Hand

The really nice thing about this method of appliqué, is that once the appliqué pieces are glued to the background, there is no need for pins to hold them in place; this makes the process of hand stitching them easier. To stitch by hand, simply use a thin thread (we like the Superior® Threads Bottom Line) that is close in color to your appliqué piece, and sew using a blind stitch, fig. 13, p. 14. You want to keep nice small even stitches, with your stitches grabbing only a few threads of the appliqué edge.

Raw Edge Fusible Web Appliqué

This process is fast, easy and gives a soft finish to your quilt. The tracing and cutting out makes a huge difference in how your appliqué feels. Choose a lightweight, paper-backed fusible web that can be stitched through.

Refer to p. 11 under the Create a Template Section to create the templates for your appliqué shapes.

Once you have created your templates, use a pencil to trace your template shapes onto the paper side of your fusible web, fig. 14.

Cut out the traced appliqué shapes approximately ¼" outside the traced line. Do not cut directly on the line. To reduce the stiffness of the finished project, cut away the center of the fusible web shape, once again cutting approximately ¼" inside the traced lines, fig. 15.

Place the fusible web shape, paper side up, on the wrong side of the appliqué fabric. Following the manufacturer's instructions, press in place, fig. 16. Let appliqué shape cool.

Cut out the fabric shape on the drawn line, fig. 17. Peel off the paper backing and fuse to appliqué background.

Based on your preference, refer to the sections Stich Appliqué pieces by Machine or by Hand to stitch the shape to background fabric, p. 14.

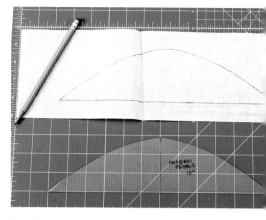

Fig. 14

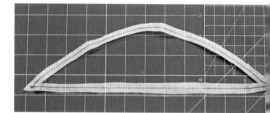

Fig. 15

Fig. 16

Fig. 17

··· Finishing the Quilt ···

Fig. 1

Fig. 2

Fig. 3

Binding Instructions

There are several ways and styles to apply a binding to enhance your style of quilt design. We chose to bind our quilts with a traditional continuous binding with mitered corners. This style of binding not only finishes the raw edges, it creates a narrow frame around the quilt. The binding will provide durability for your quilt. We like the finished binding width to be approximately ¼".

Sew the strips together, end to end, at a 45 degree angle, fig. 1. You can draw a sewing line as a guide. Trim the excess fabric from the corner, fig. 2, and press the seams open, fig. 3.

Fold the binding strip in half lengthwise with wrong sides together. Align the raw edges of the binding to the raw edge of the quilt. Starting 8" from the end of the binding, sew a scant ¼" seam. Stop sewing ¼" from the corner and backstitch, fig. 4.

Fig. 4

Appliqué for MODERN Beginners ✦ *Eva Birch, Nancy Gano, & Jodi Robinson*

Remove quilt from machine, fold binding up forming a 45 degree angle, fig. 5.

Fold the binding back down over the 45 degree angle to align the back to the second edge, fig. 6. Start sewing ¼" from corner, backstitch, and continue in same manner along all sides of quilt.

When you reach the beginning of the binding, fold over the tail end of the binding, until the fold lines up with the raw end of beginning strip, fig. 7. From the fold, measure the width of your binding strip (2¼"), fig. 8, and trim the excess tail of binding, fig. 9. Open both ends of the binding, lay right sides together, using the same method as joining strips in the very beginning, sew together at a 45 degree, trim excess fabric from corner, press seam open and finish stitching to quilt, fig. 10.

Fold the binding to the back of the quilt, and use a small blind stitch to hand sew the binding down. Fold the corners in one at a time and secure with a couple of additional stitches.

Fig. 5

Fig. 6

Fig. 7

Fig. 8

Fig. 9

Fig. 10

Hanging Sleeve

Making and attaching a hanging sleeve to a quilt is an easy procedure. The hanging sleeve, a pocket attached to the back side of a quilt, allows a rod to be inserted across the quilt back to hang the quilt for display. The hanging sleeve runs the width of the quilt. Depth can vary according to taste, preferences, or show requirements. Any type of fabric can be used to make the sleeve such as coordinating fabric or a muslin.

Making the Sleeve

✦ Measure the width of your quilt. Cut a piece of fabric the same width as your quilt by 8½" deep. This will make a 4" deep finished sleeve.

✦ Finish the ends of the sleeve by folding the raw edges over twice, iron the fold, then stitch a seam with a ¼" seam along the fold.

✦ Fold the sleeve in half lengthwise with the wrong sides and raw edges together. Iron along the fold, making a well-defined crease. Open the crease and then fold the long raw edges in to meet at the center crease. Iron the new fold lines. Place right sides together and pin.

✦ Sew along the edge, using a ¼" seam. When finished, turn the sleeve right side out. The hanging sleeve will look like a "D" when viewed from the side. This is correct and allows room for a display rod to be easily inserted.

Attach Hanging Sleeve to Quilt

✦ Pin the hanging sleeve to the quilt back ½" below the top edge of the quilt. To precisely measure the mark on the seam line use a measuring tape and chalk or pencil.

✦ Hand stitch the top and bottom sides of the sleeve to the quilt back using loose, overhand stitches or long, running stitches. Ensure the stitches cannot be seen on the front side of the quilt.

✦ Hand stitch the sleeve side edges to the quilt back, using small stitches a ¹⁄₁₆" to ⅛" apart. A secure side seam will prevent a hanging rod being improperly inserted behind the sleeve and causing damage to your quilt backing. Your quilt is now ready to be hung and displayed.

Label Your Quilt

You have just created a beautiful piece of work, now put a label on it! This can be as simple as a piece of muslin with freezer paper on the back, for ease in writing, with a fine-tip permanent marker and hand stitched to quilt back. The label should, at a minimum, include the name of your quilt, your name, date it was made, and what town it was made in. The label could be created out of a leftover block, an embroidered label, fabric sheets for printer or even a painted label. Include recipients name and occasion for which it was made. Future generations will be happy to learn the history of your quilt.

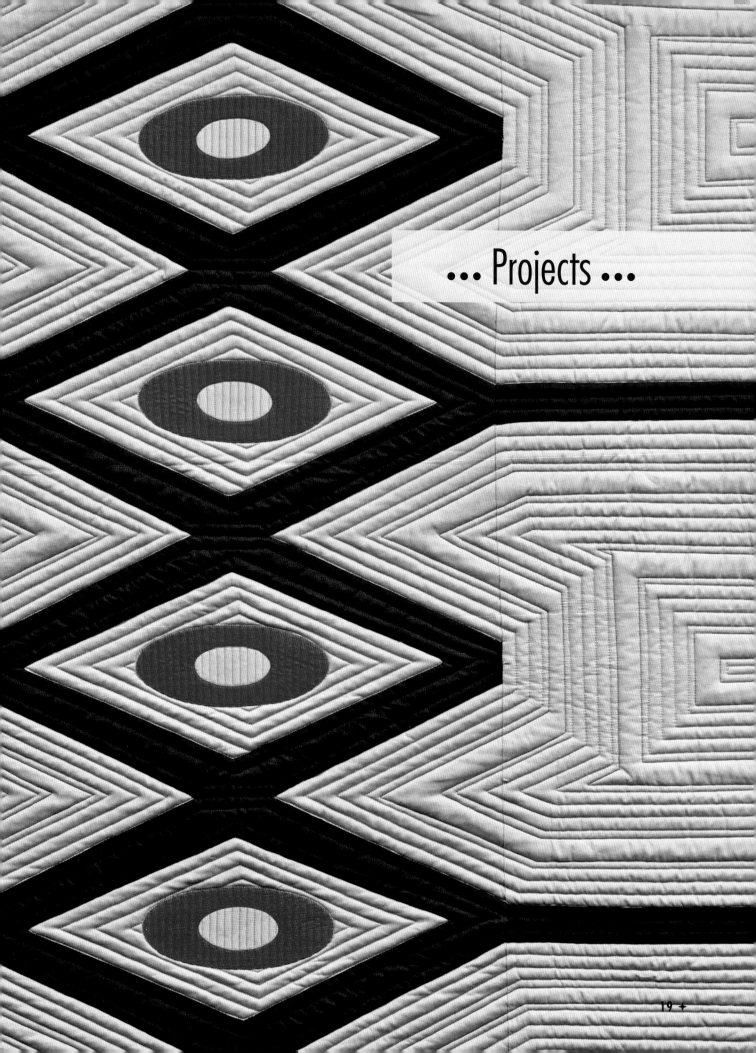

... Projects ...

AT THE CABIN, 48" x 56". Designed, pieced, and quilted by Jodi Robinson

AT THE CABIN

48" x 56"

Fabric Requirements

Red – Fat quarter
Green – Fat quarter
Yellow – Fat quarter
Light Taupe – ¾ yard
Medium Taupe – ¾ yard
Dark Taupe – ¾ yard
Cream – 2½ yards *(includes binding)*
Backing – 3 yards
Fusible web or appliqué interfacing for
your chosen appliqué method

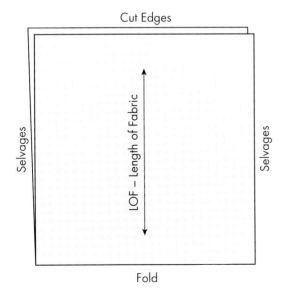

Fig. 1

Cutting
Cream

NOTE: You will be cutting the Cream fabric by the LOF (length of fabric), NOT by the WOF (width of fabric). Before cutting strips, fold the 2½ yards of fabric in half lengthwise, with the cut edges together and the selvage edges on both sides, fig. 1.

Cut two (2) 8½" x LOF strips
    Subcut one (1) strip into
    One (1) 8½" x 56½" rectangle
    One (1) 8½" x 24½" rectangle

    Subcut one (1) strip into
    Two (2) 8½" x 24½" rectangles
    Two (2) 8½" x 16½" rectangles

Cut one (1) 16½" x LOF strip
    Subcut one (1) 16½" x 56½" rectangle

Cut three (3) 2¼" x LOF strips (binding)

Light Taupe

Cut two (2) 8½" x WOF strips
    Subcut three (3) 8½" x 8½" squares
    One (1) 8½" x 24½" rectangle

Medium Taupe

Cut two (2) 8½" x WOF strips
    Subcut four (4) 8½" x 8½" squares
    One (1) 8½" x 16½" rectangle

Dark Taupe

Cut two (2) 8½" x WOF strips
    Subcut four (4) 8½" x 8½" squares
    One (1) 8½"x 4½" rectangle
    One (1) 8½" x 12½" rectangle

Fig. 2

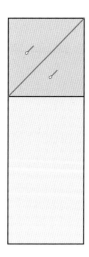

Fig. 3

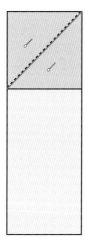

Fig. 4

Assembly

Stitch and Flip Technique *(you will use this technique to create the appliqué background sections)*

Using the marking tool of your choice (I use a regular pencil to mark a light line), mark a diagonal line from corner to corner on the wrong side of your fabric square, fig. 2.

To create the appliqué background sections you will align your diagonally marked squares on top of the Cream background piece, right sides together, and pin in place on each side of the diagonal line, fig. 3.

You will now use the marked diagonal line as your sewing guide. You want to sew about a threads width away from the marked line, on the side that will be trimmed away, fig. 4.

Trim the corner ¼" from your sewn line. Flip remaining fabric out, and press seam allowance towards the outside, figs. 5a–c.

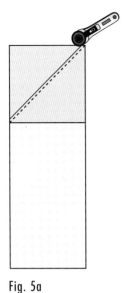

Fig. 5a

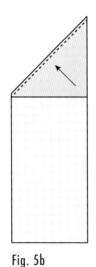

Fig. 5b

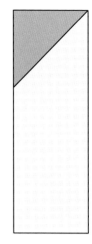

Fig. 5c

When assembling the appliqué background sections, it is very important that you align and sew your pieces as shown in the illustrations. You will use the stitch and flip technique at both ends of your Cream rectangles to create these sections.

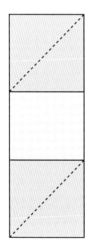

Fig. 6a

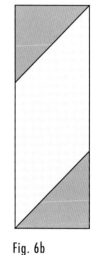

Fig. 6b

Using one (1) Cream 8½" x 24½" rectangle and two (2) Light Taupe 8½" x 8½" squares, create one (1) appliqué background section, figs. 6a–b.

Using one (1) 8½" x 24½" and one (1) 8½" x 16½" Cream rectangle and four (4) Dark Taupe 8½" x 8½" squares, create one (1) large, figs. 7a–b and one (1) small appliqué background section, figs. 7c–d.

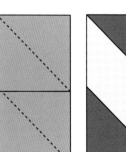

Fig. 7a   Fig. 7b   Fig. 7c   Fig. 7d

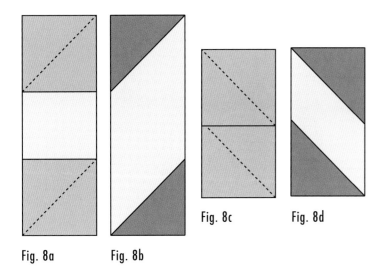

Fig. 8a   Fig. 8b   Fig. 8c   Fig. 8d

Using one (1) 8½" x 24½" and one (1) 8½" x 16½" Cream rectangle and four (4) Medium Taupe 8½" x 8½" squares, create one (1) large, figs. 8a–b and one (1) small appliqué background section figs. 8c–d.

Using your chosen appliqué technique, prepare your appliqué shapes, pp. 28–29.

NOTE: The shapes are directional, so you will need to reverse the template when tracing some of your appliqué pieces. I have notated on the templates which colors will be a reverse images.

You will need:

Two (2) Large Green shapes one (1) of these will be a reverse image of the template

One (1) Large Red shape which will be a reverse image of the template

One (1) Small Red shape which will be a reverse image of the template

One (1) Small Yellow shape

Referring to the instructions on p. 13 (centering appliqués in the Appliqué Methods section), center your prepared appliqué pieces on the appliqué backgrounds you created. Refer to the final quilt assembly diagram, p. 26, for color placement. Sew or fuse appliqué shapes in place.

For quilt assembly, refer to the assembly diagram, p. 25, to create the three (3) individual center columns. You will then join the completed columns together into one unit. The last step is to attach the two (2) large Cream pieces to the right and left sides as shown.

Quilt as desired, or as shown in the provided quilting diagram, p. 27. Bind using the provided instructions on pp. 16–17 (Finishing the Quilt section), or by using your favorite binding method.

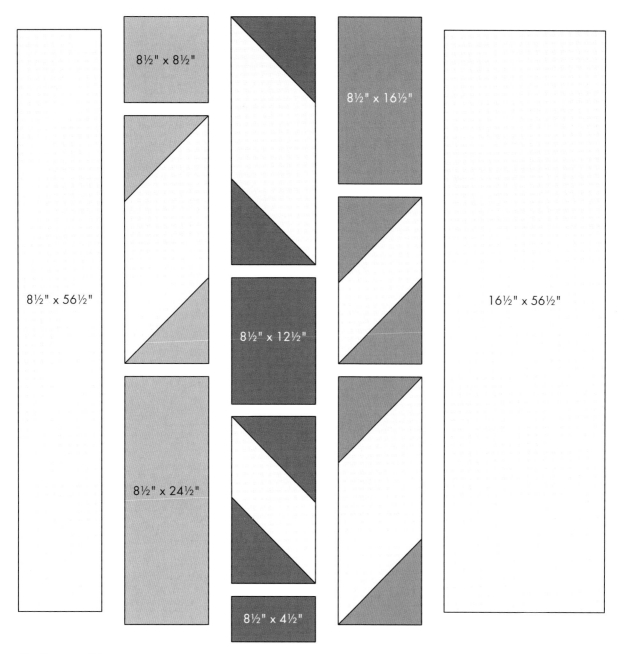

8½" x 8½"

8½" x 56½"

8½" x 16½"

8½" x 12½"

8½" x 24½"

16½" x 56½"

8½" x 4½"

Quilt assembly

Final quilt assembly

Quilting diagram

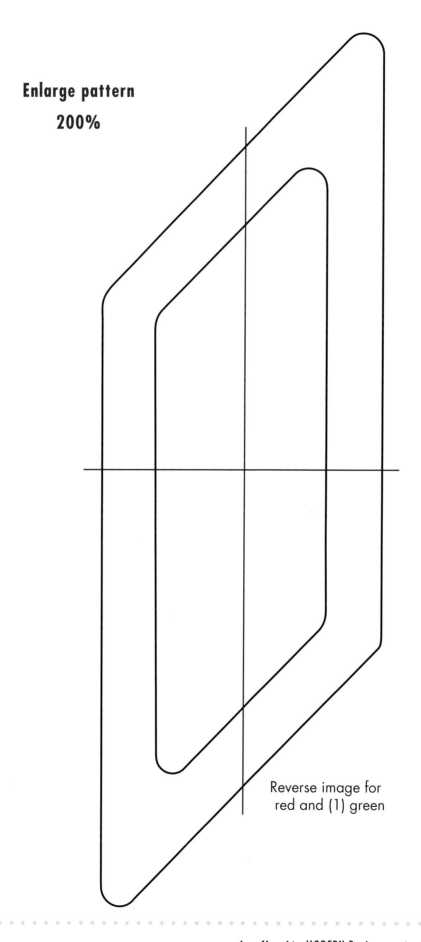

**Enlarge pattern
200%**

Reverse image for
red and (1) green

Appliqué for MODERN Beginners ✦ *Eva Birch, Nancy Gano, & Jodi Robinson*

**Enlarge pattern
200%**

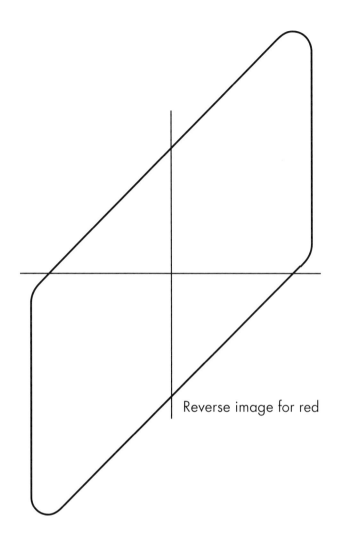

Reverse image for red

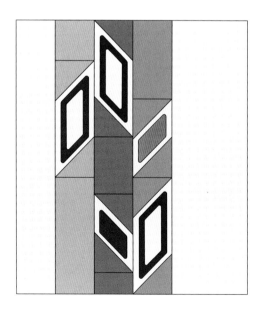

CONFIGURATION, 50" x 63". Designed, pieced, and quilted by Eva Birch

CONFIGURATION

50" x 63"

Fabric Requirements

Gray – 3½ yards *(includes binding)*

Pink – ¾ yard

Magenta – 1 yard

Blue – 1 Fat quarter

Backing – 3½ yard

Fusible web or appliqué interfacing for
your chosen appliqué method

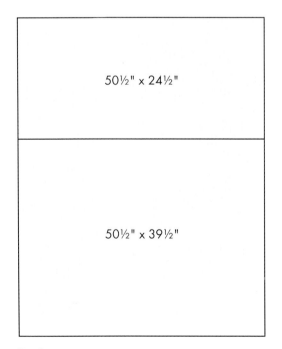

Fig. 1

Cutting

Gray

Cut six (6) 2¼" x WOF strips for binding

Cut two (2) 50½" x WOF strips
Subcut one (1) 50½" x 24½" rectangle
One (1) 50½" x 39½" rectangle

Assembly

Using your chosen method for appliqué,
prepare your appliqué shapes, p. 35.

Nine (9) 3" Blue circles
Twelve (12) 6" x 12" Pink petals
Eight (8) 6" x 12" Magenta petals

Sew the Gray 50½" x 24½" rectangle to
the Gray 50½" x 38½" rectangle, fig. 1.

This 50½" x 64" piece is your background
on which you will glue/fuse your appliqué
shapes.

As shown in the included diagram, fig.
2, p. 32, draw a grid, using the finished petal
size as a guide. This will help you to place
the petals with ease and to assure proper
placement and accuracy of the design.

Center the circle shapes as shown in the diagram, fig. 2.

Sew or fuse in place.

Quilt as desired or as shown in the quilting diagram, p. 33.

Bind using the provided instructions on pp. 16–17 (Finishing the Quilt section), or by using your favorite binding method.

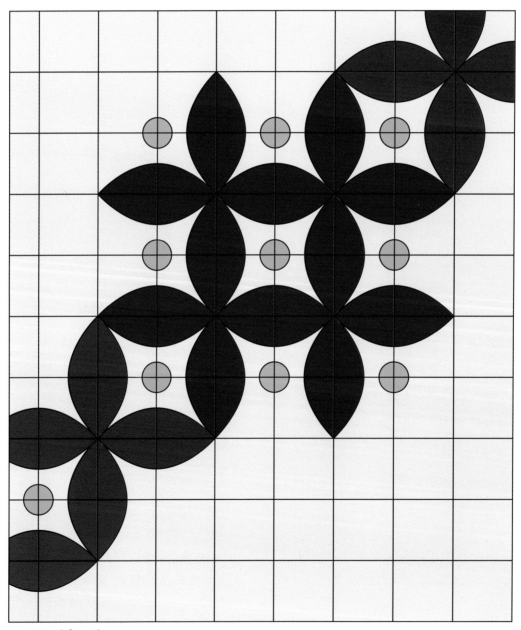

Fig. 2. Grid for placement

Quilting diagram

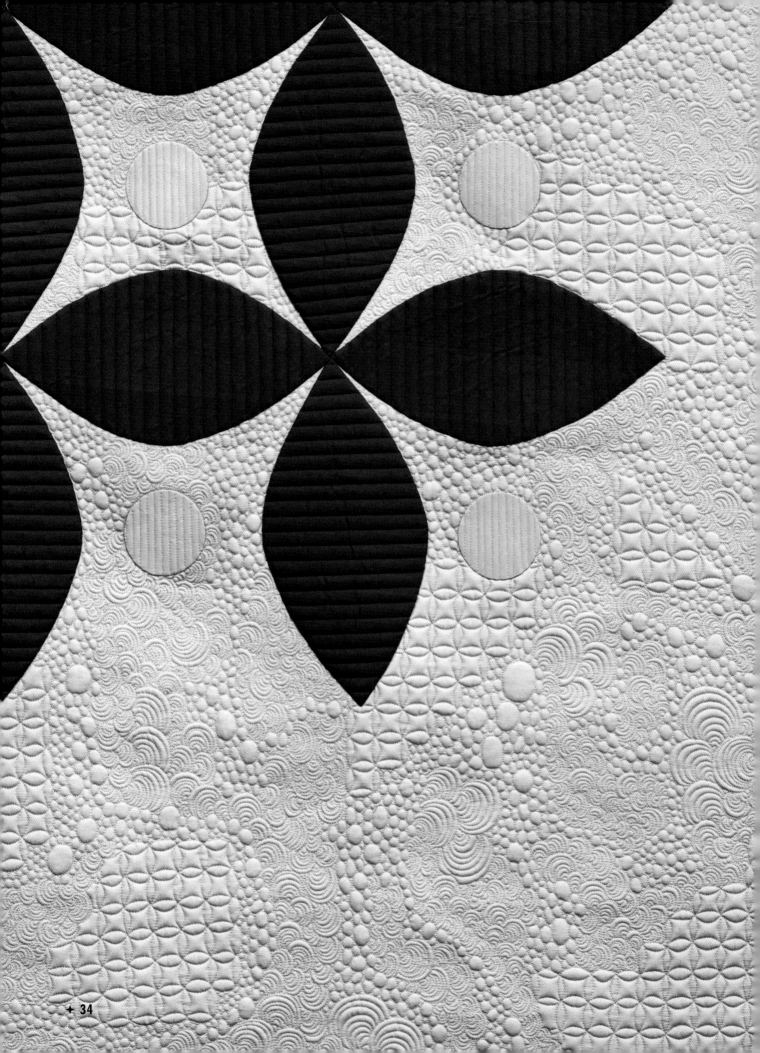

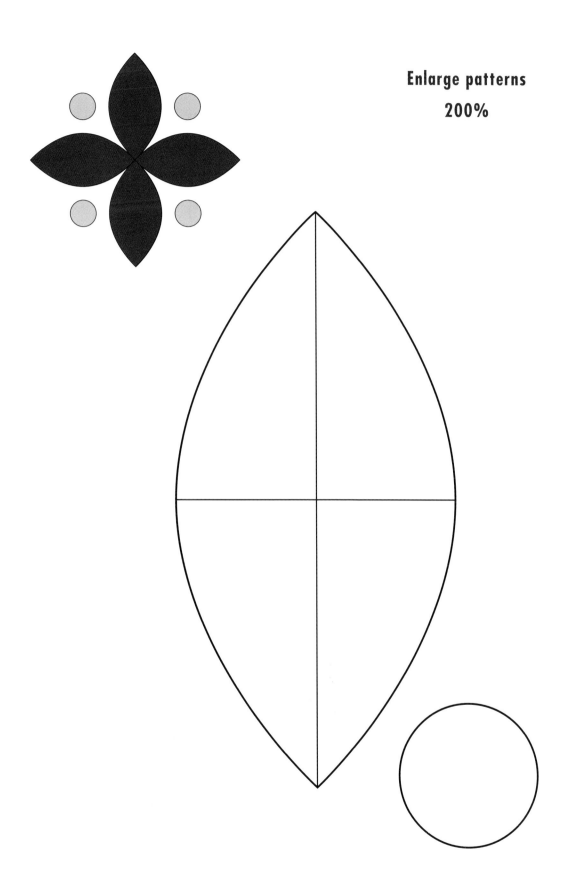

**Enlarge patterns
200%**

INTERCHANGE, 72" x 72". Designed, pieced, and quilted by Jodi Robinson

Appliqué for MODERN Beginners ✦ *Eva Birch, Nancy Gano, & Jodi Robinson*

INTERCHANGE

72" x 72"

Fabric Requirements

White – 2 yards
Orange – 1 yard
Gray – 4 yards *(includes binding)*
Backing – 5 yards
Fusible web or appliqué interfacing for
  your chosen appliqué method

Cutting

White

Cut one (1) 2½" x WOF strip
  Subcut eight (8) 2½" squares
  Four (4) 2½" x 4½" rectangles

Cut three (3) 8½" x WOF strips
  From one (1) of the strips
  subcut two (2) 20½" pieces

Cut one (1) 32½" piece from each of the
  remaining two (2) strips (you will have
  extra left from each strip)

Cut two (2) 12½" x WOF strips
  Subcut four (4) 12½" squares (there
    will be extra left from each strip)

Orange

Cut one (1) 4½" x WOF strip
  Subcut eight (8) 4½" squares

Cut six (6) 2½" x WOF strips
  Subcut one (1) 32½" piece
  One (1) 4½" piece from four (4) of the
    strips
  Subcut two (2) 20½" pieces from
    two (2) of the strips

Cut one (1) 9" x WOF strip
  Subcut four (4) 9" squares (for appliqué
    shapes)

Gray

Cut three (3) 4½" x WOF strips
  Subcut twenty-four (24) 4½" squares

NOTE: You can use the extra leftover
fabric for your appliqué circles.

Cut four (4) 12½" x WOF strips
  From each of two (2) strips
  subcut one (1) 12½" square
  one (1) 24½" piece

  From each of the remaining two (2)
    strips cut one (1) 36½" piece

Cut two (2) 24½" x WOF strips
> From one (1) strip subcut one (1) 24½" square
>
> from the remaining strip subcut one (1) 24½" x 36½" piece

Cut eight (8) 2¼" x WOF strips (these will be used for binding)

Fig. 1

Assembly

Using four (4) 9" Orange squares and Gray scraps, prepare your appliqué shapes, p. 43, using the appliqué method you prefer.

Center your appliqué shapes on the four (4) 12½" x 12½" White background squares. Refer to instructions for centering your shapes on p. 13 (in the Appliqué Methods section), fuse or stitch your shapes in place.

After fusing/sewing your appliqué shapes, use sixteen (16) 4½" x 4½" squares to add the Gray corners to your appliqué blocks using the stitch and flip technique (refer to pp. 22–24 for stitch and flip technique instructions).

Fig. 2

Next, create the two (2) long and two (2) short Orange and White units. Use four (4) 4½" x 2½" White rectangles and four (4) 4½" x 2½" Orange rectangles make four (4) units, fig. 1.

Using eight (8) 4½" x 4½" Orange squares, eight (8) 4½" x 4½" Gray squares, and eight (8) 2½" x 2½" White squares, make eight (8) stitch and flip blocks, fig. 2. Refer to pp. 22–24 for stitch and flip technique instructions.

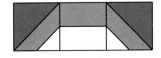

Fig. 3

> NOTE: You will apply the stitch and flip technique to two (2) opposite corners of each Orange square, as shown.

Make four (4) end units as shown, fig. 3, p. 38.

Using four (4) 32½" x 2½" Orange strips and two (2) 32½" x 8½" White rectangles make two (2) long units as shown, fig. 4.

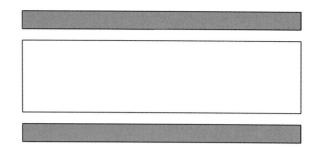

Fig. 4

Using four (4) 20½" x 2½" Orange strips and two (2) 20½" x 8½" White rectangles make two (2) short units as shown, fig. 5.

Complete the assembly of the two (2) long and two (2) short Orange and White units by sewing one (1) end unit to each of the long and short White and Orange sections as shown, figs. 6a–6b.

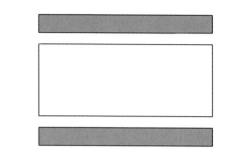

Fig. 5

Referring to the Assembly Diagram, piece each of (5) individual units as shown, p. 40.

After constructing the (5) individual units, refer to the Final Quilt Assembly Diagram, p. 41 to complete your quilt top. Sew units 1, 2, and 3 together first to make the top half of the quilt. Then sew units 4 and 5 together to make the bottom half of the quilt. The final step is to sew the top and bottom sections together.

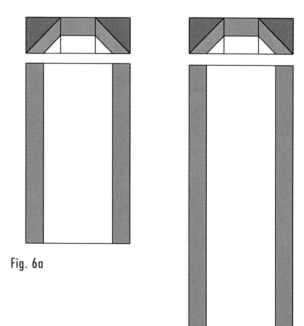

Fig. 6a

Fig. 6b

Quilt as desired, or as shown on the provided quilting diagram, p. 42. Bind using the provided instructions on pp. 16–17 (Finishing the Quilt section), or by using your favorite binding method.

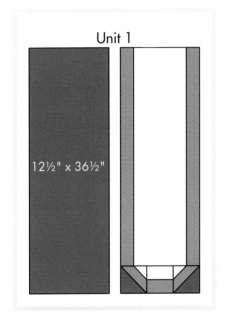

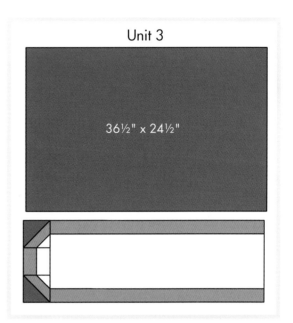

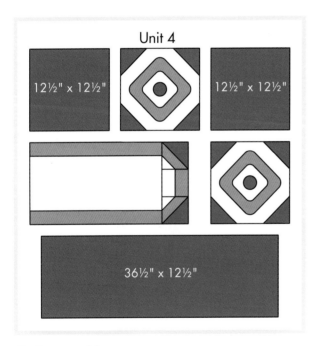

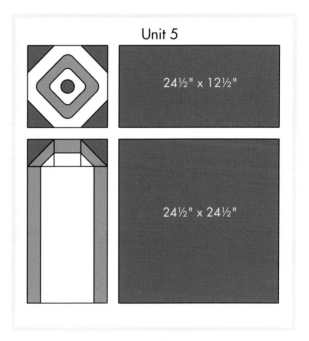

Quilt assembly

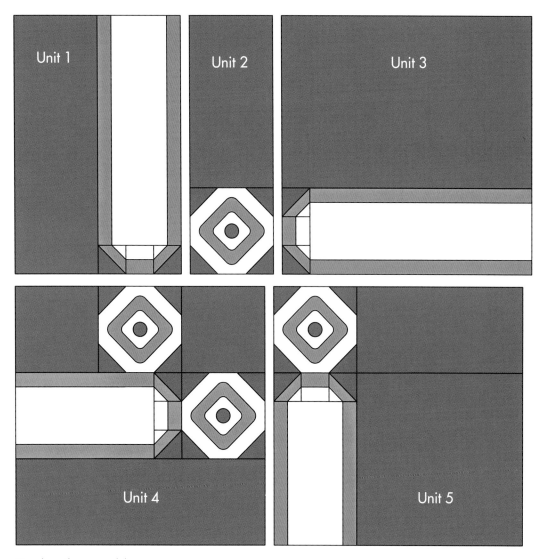

Final quilt assembly

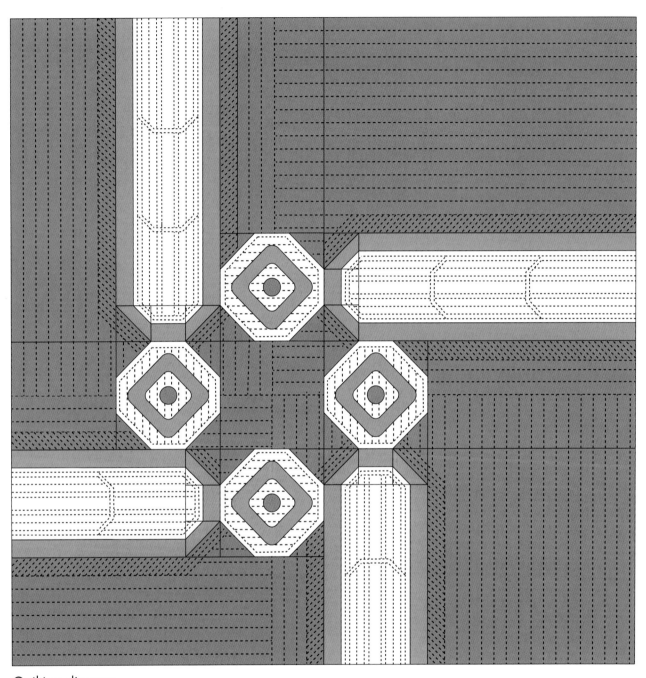

Quilting diagram

Enlarge patterns
200%

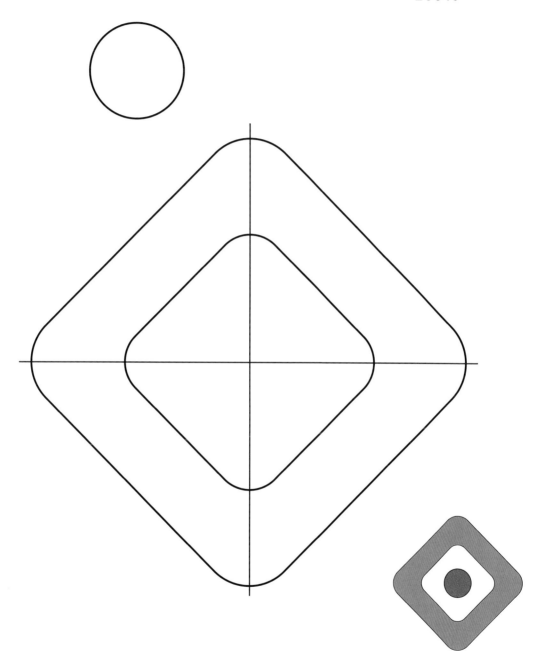

METRO, 20" x 40". Designed, pieced, and quilted by Eva Birch

Appliqué for MODERN Beginners + *Eva Birch, Nancy Gano, & Jodi Robinson*

METRO

20" x 40"

Fabric Requirements

Light Gray – 1 yard background (*includes binding*)

Dark Gray – ¼ yard accent

Blue/Teal – 1 fat quarter

Magenta – 1 fat quarter

Backing fabric – 1 yard

Fusible web or appliqué interfacing for your chosen appliqué method

Cutting

Light Gray

Cut one (1) 20½" x WOF strip

    Subcut into one (1) 20½" x 3½" strip

        One (1) 20½" x 16½" rectangle

        One (1) 20½" x 19½" rectangle

Cut four (4) 2¼" strips WOF for binding

Dark Gray

Cut one (1) 1½" x WOF strip

Subcut into two (2) 1½" x 20½" pieces

Assembly

Using your chosen appliqué technique, prepare your appliqué shapes, p. 49.

Four (4) Blue/Teal hexagon shapes
Three (3) Magenta circle shapes

Referring to the instructions on p. 13 (how to center appliqué shapes), center your three (3) prepared Magenta circles onto the three (3) Blue/Teal hexagon shapes.

Cut one (1) of the three (3) Hexagon/Circle shapes in half.

Cut the remaining Hexagon shape into ¼'s, using the final quilt assembly diagram, p. 47, for reference.

Referring to the instructions on p. 13, center your prepared appliqué pieces on the 16½" x 20½" Light Gray rectangle.

Sew or fuse in place.

Referring to the quilt assembly diagram, p. 47, sew both 20½" x 1½" Dark Gray strips to each long side of the 20½" x 16½" appliqué section.

Sew one (1) 20½" x 3½" Light Gray strip to one side of the unit.

Sew one (1) 20½" x 19½" Light Gray rectangle to the other side of the unit.

Quilt as desired, or as shown in the provided quilting diagram, p. 48.

Bind using the provided instructions on pp. 16–17 (Finishing the Quilt section), or by using your favorite binding method.

20½" x 3½"

20½" x 1½"

20½" x 16½"

20½" x 1½"

20½" x 19½"

Quilt assembly

Final quilt assembly

Quilting diagram

Enlarge pattern

200%

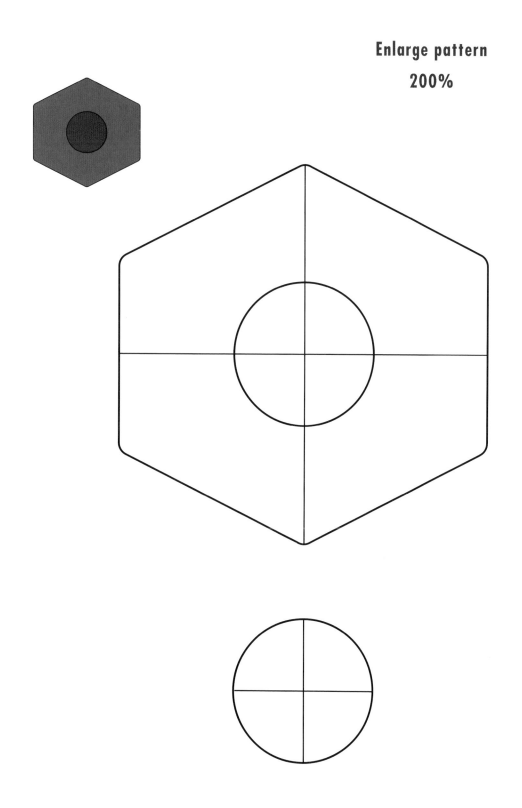

MODERN PETALS, 50" x 60". Designed, pieced, and quilted by Nancy Gano

MODERN PETALS

50" x 60"

Fabric Requirements

Light Green – 2¾ yards *(background, light appliqué petals, binding)*

Dark Green – ¼ yard *(dark appliqué petals)*

Magenta – 1 yard *(appliqué background and partial frame inset)*

Purple – Three (3) ¾ yard assorted shades *(appliqué background)*

Backing – 3½ yards

Fusible web or appliqué interfacing for your chosen appliqué method

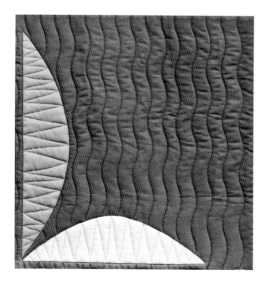

Cutting

Light Green:

Cut three (3) 4½" x WOF strips

Sew three (3) 4½" x WOF Light Green strips together, end to end.

Subcut strip into one (1) 4½" x 32½" strip

Subcut one (1) 4½" x 46½" strip

Cut three (3) 6½" x WOF strips

Sew three (3) 6½" x WOF Light Green strips together, end to end.

Subcut into one (1) 6½" x 44½" strip

Subcut one (1) 6½" x 60½" strip

Cut one (1) 7" x WOF strip for appliqué petals

Cut one (1) 8½" x WOF strip

Subcut one (1) 8½" x 32½" strip

Cut two(2) 12½" x WOF strips

Sew two (2) 12½" x WOF Light Green strips together, end to end.

Subcut one (1) 12½" x 44½" rectangle

Cut six (6) 2¼" x WOF strips (binding)

Dark Green:

Cut one (1) 7" x WOF strip for appliqué petals

Magenta

Cut one (1) 16½" x WOF strip
  Subcut one (1) 16½" x 16½" square

Cut two (2) 2½" x WOF strips
  Sew two (2) 2½" x WOF Magenta strips together, end to end.
  Subcut one (1) 2½" x 44½" strip

Cut two (2) 4½" x WOF strips
  Sew two (2) 4½" x WOF Magenta strips together, end to end.
  Subcut one (1) 4½" x 44½" strip

Cut one (1) 16½" x WOF strip
  Subcut one (1) 16½" x 16½" square

Purple

Cut one (1) 16½" x WOF strip for each shade
  Subcut one (1) 16½" x 16½" square

Assembly

Prepare your appliqué shapes, p. 56, using the appliqué method you prefer. Create the appliqué units on the Magenta and Purple backgrounds. Refer to the final quilt assembly diagram, p. 54, for appliqué placement. Each appliqué petal should be placed ¾" in from raw edges, leaving a small space between tips in corner. Sew the four (4) petal appliqué units together according to quilt assembly diagram, p. 53. Press seams open.

Refer to the quilt assembly diagram, p. 53 to add the outer Green and Magenta strips.

Quilt as desired, or as shown in the provided quilting diagram, p. 55. Bind using the provided instructions on pp. 16–17 or your favorite binding method.

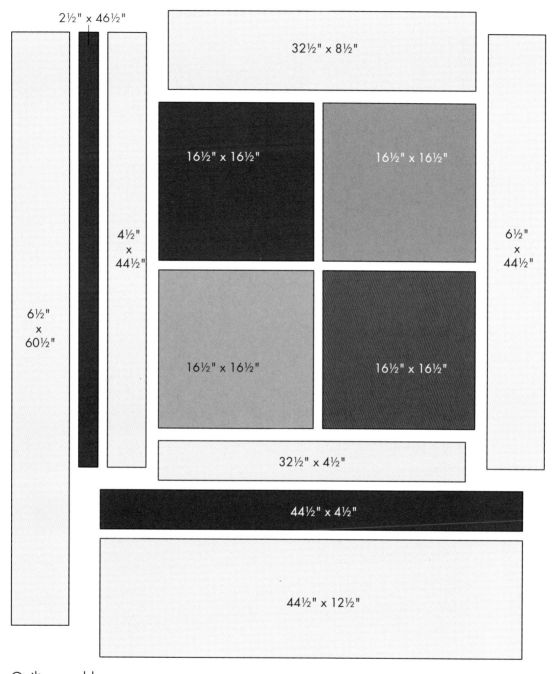

2½" x 46½"

32½" x 8½"

16½" x 16½"

16½" x 16½"

4½"
x
44½"

6½"
x
44½"

6½"
x
60½"

16½" x 16½"

16½" x 16½"

32½" x 4½"

44½" x 4½"

44½" x 12½"

Quilt assembly

Final quilt assembly

Quilting diagram

**Enlarge patterns
200%**

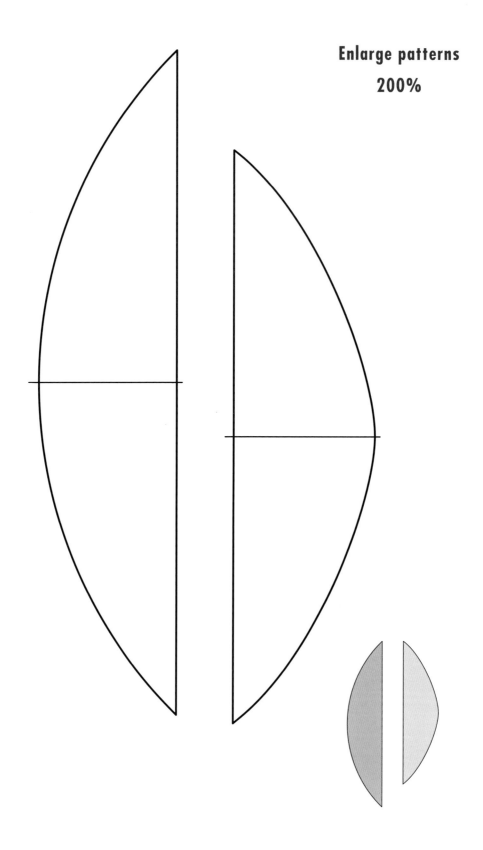

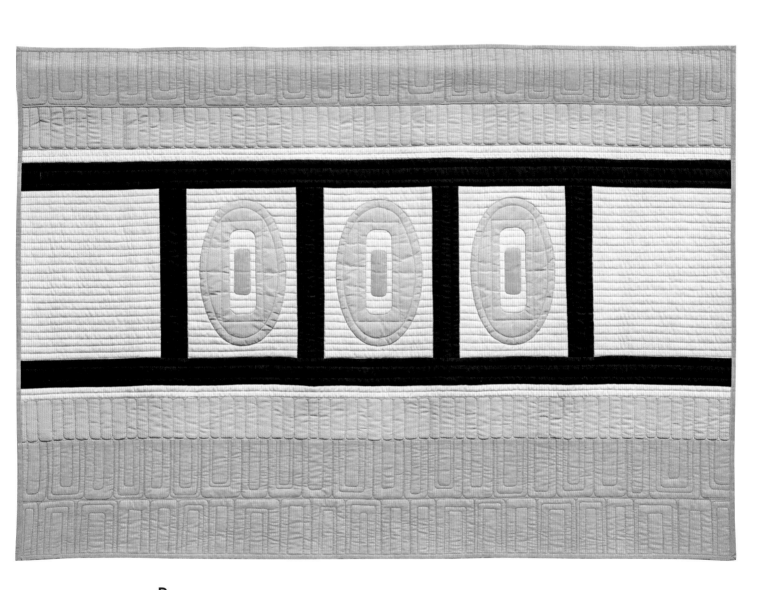

Pᴀᴛʜᴡᴀʏ 36" x 52". Designed, pieced, and quilted by Jodi Robinson

PATHWAY

36" x 52"

Fabric Requirements

Brown – ½ yard *(sashing strips)*

Green – ¾ yard

Beige – 1 yard

Yellow – 2 yards *(includes binding)*

Backing fabric – 1¾ yards

Fusible web or appliqué interfacing for
your chosen appliqué method

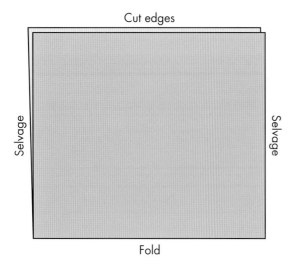

Fig. 1

Cutting

Brown

Cut five (5) 2½" x WOF strips
Subcut four (4) 12½" x 2½" rectangles
(you will use two (2) of the strips
for this)

Green

Cut one (1) 8" x WOF
Subcut three (3) 12" x 8" rectangles (for
appliqué shapes)

Cut three (3) 3½" x WOF strips

Beige

Cut one (1) 10½" x WOF strip
Subcut two (2) 10½" x 12½" rectangles

Cut one (1) 8½" x WOF strip
Subcut three (3) 8½" x 12½" rectangles
(appliqué backgrounds)

Cut three (3) 1½" x WOF strips

Yellow

NOTE: You will be cutting the Yellow
fabric LOF (length of fabric), NOT WOF.
Before cutting strips, fold the 2 yards of
fabric with the cut edges together, and
selvage edges on both sides, fig. 1.

Cut three (3) 2¼" x LOF strips (for binding)

Cut one (1) 4½" x LOF strip
    Subcut one (1) 4½" x 52½" strip

Cut one (1) 8½" x LOF strip
    Subcut one (1) 8½" x 52½" strip

*Use extra fabric from your strips for the Yellow appliqué
    pieces

Assembly

Using your chosen method for appliqué, prepare your appliqué shapes, p. 63, using the three (3) 12" x 8" Green rectangles, and Yellow scraps.

Referring to the instructions on p. 13, center your prepared appliqué pieces on the three (3) 8½" x 12½" Beige rectangles. Sew or fuse in place.

Referring to the final quilt assembly diagram, p. 61, sew together the center appliqué section.

Sew three (3) 2½" x WOF Brown strips together end to end. From this long piece cut two (2) 52½" strips. Attach these pieces to the top and bottom of the center appliqué section as shown in final quilt assembly diagram, p. 61.

Sew three (3) 1½" x WOF Beige strips together end to end. From this long strip cut two (2) 52½" strips.

Sew three (3) 3½" x WOF Green strips together end to end. From this long strip cut two (2) 52½" strips.

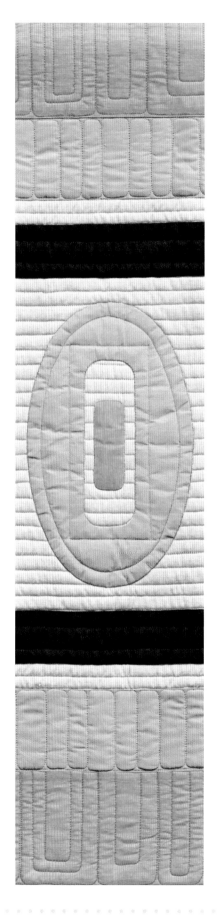

Referring to the quilt assembly diagram, piece the top and bottom sections. You will sew together one (1) each of the long 52½" strips of Beige, Green, and Yellow to form each unit. You will make two (2) of these units.

Attach the top and bottom strip units to the center appliqué section to complete your quilt.

Quilt as desired, or as shown in the provided quilting diagram, p. 62. Bind using the provided instructions on pp. 16–17 (Finishing the Quilt) or your favorite binding method.

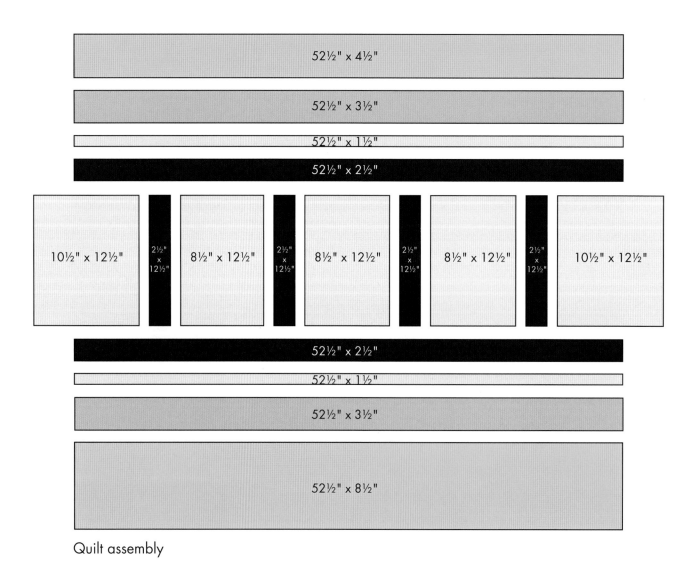

Quilt assembly

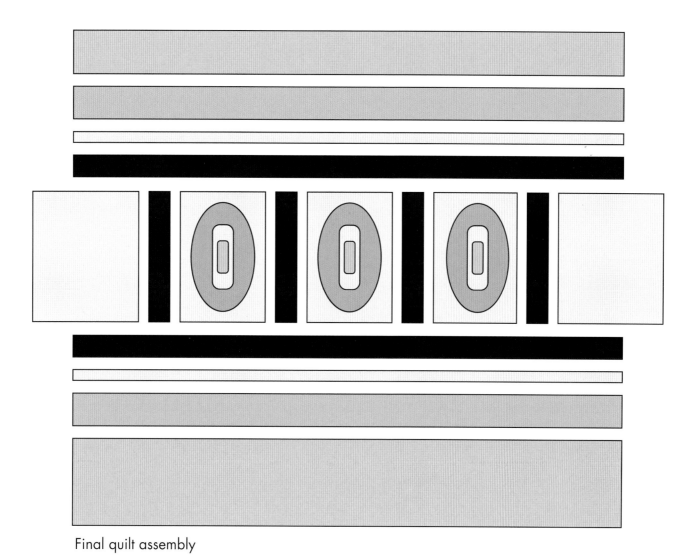

Final quilt assembly

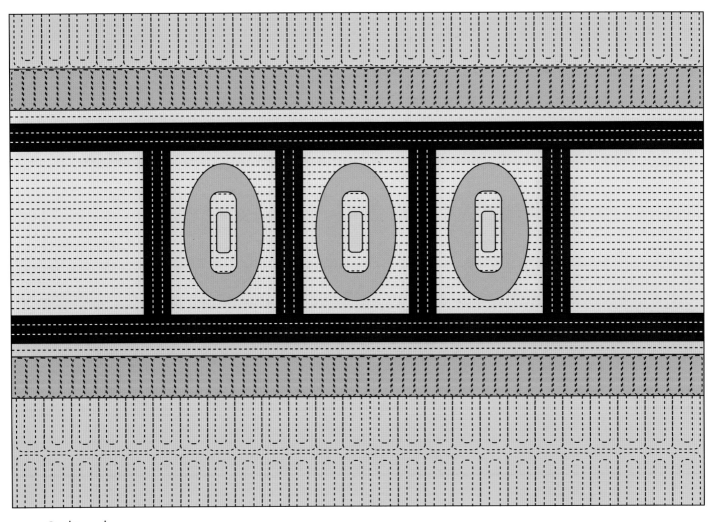

Quilting diagram

Enlarge patterns
200%

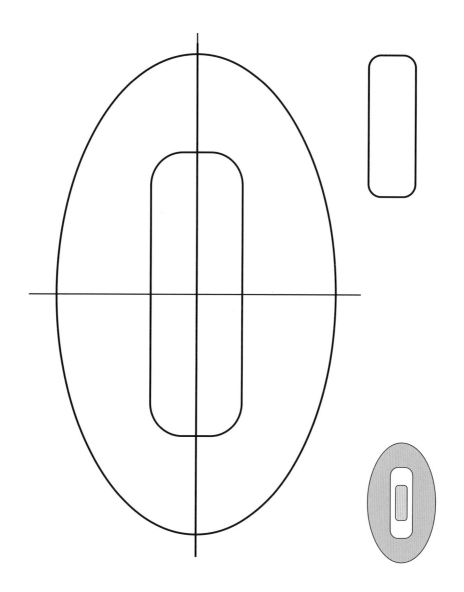

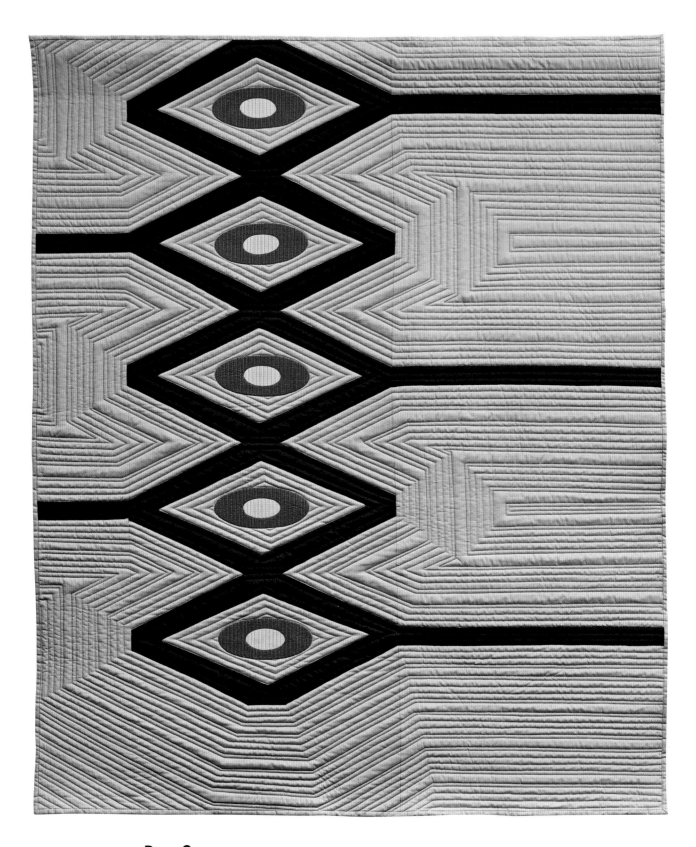

RUN-OFF, 50" x 63". Designed, pieced, and quilted by Eva Birch

Appliqué for MODERN Beginners ✦ *Eva Birch, Nancy Gano, & Jodi Robinson*

RUN-OFF

50" x 63"

Fabric Requirements

Tan – 4 yards
Brown – 1½ yards
Orange – 1 Fat quarter
Yellow – 1 Fat quarter
Backing Fabric – 3½ yards
Fusible web or appliqué interfacing for
   your chosen appliqué method

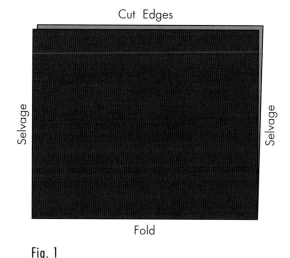

Cut Edges

Selvage

Selvage

Fold

Fig. 1

Cutting

Tan

Cut six (6) 2¼" x WOF strips (binding)

Cut two (2) 21½" x WOF rectangles
   Subcut two (2) 20" x 21½" rectangles,
      One (1) 14" x 21½" rectangle
      One (1) 5½" x 21½" strip

Cut two (2) 8½" x 25" strips
   Subcut (1) 25" x 8½" strip
      One (1) 15½" x 8½" rectangle
      One (1) 20½" x 8½" strip

Cut one (1) 21½" x 63½" rectangle
   (appliqué background)

NOTE: You can overcut the width of this
piece and trim to size after you appliqué
your shapes on the background fabric.

Brown

Cut three (3) 2½" x WOF strips
   Subcut three (3) 2½" x 21½" strips
      Two (2) 2½" x 8" strips

The remainder of the brown fabric is
used to make your five (5) diamond appliqué
shapes as referred to on p. 11.

Assembly

Using your chosen method for appliqué, prepare your appliqué shapes, p. 70, using the Brown, Orange, and Yellow fabrics.

Make five (5) shapes from each fabric.

Center, then sew or fuse the Yellow appliqué shapes onto the Orange appliqué shapes. Set these five (5) units aside.

Referring to the instructions on p. 13 center your five (5) prepared Brown diamond appliqué shapes on the 21½" x 63" rectangle (or your over cut) Tan appliqué background piece.

Then center the five (5) Orange/Yellow appliqué units within the five (5) Brown diamond shape, following the final quilt assembly diagram, p. 68.

Fuse or sew in place.

Following the quilt assembly diagram, p. 67, sew the following strips together to form the side units.

Side 1

Sew one (1) Tan 8½" x 15½" rectangle to one (1) Brown 8½" x 2½" strip
Continue with one (1) Tan 8½" x 20½" rectangle
Continue with one (1) Brown 8½" x 2½" strip
Continue with one (1) Tan 8½" x 25" rectangle

Side 2

Sew one (1) Tan 21½" x 5½" strip to one (1) Brown 21½" x 2½" strip
Continue with one (1) Tan 21½" x 20" rectangle
Continue with one (1) Brown 21½" x 2½" strip
Continue with one (1) Tan 21½" x 20" rectangle
Continue with one (1) Brown 21½" x 2½" strip
Continue with one (1) Tan 21½" x 14" rectangle

Now your two (2) side units are complete.

If you overcut your appliqué background piece, measure and trim to 21½" x 63½", making sure that the Tan background fabric allows for ¼" seam allowance where the side units will be attached.

Sew the two (2) side units to the appliqué unit, making sure to match the Brown strips to the Brown diamond appliqués to ensure that the design looks continuous.

Quilt as desired or as shown in the provided quilting diagram, p. 69.

Bind using the provided instructions on pp. 16–17 (Finishing the Quilt) or your favorite binding method.

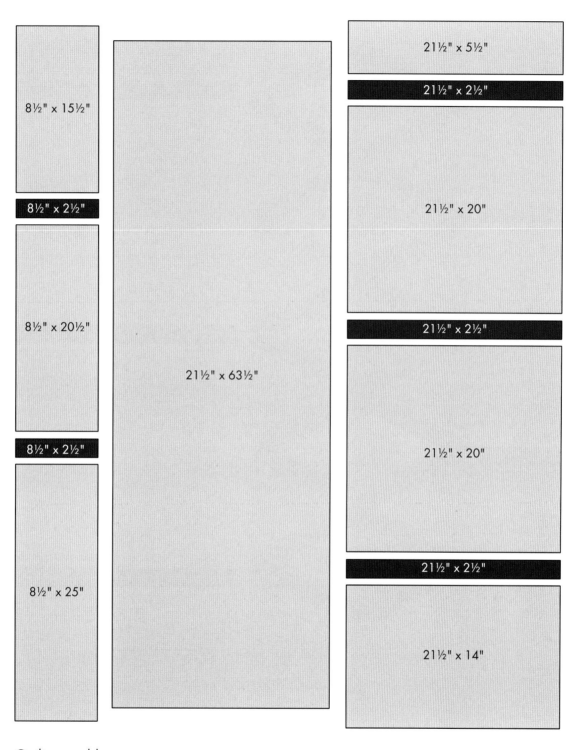

Quilt assembly

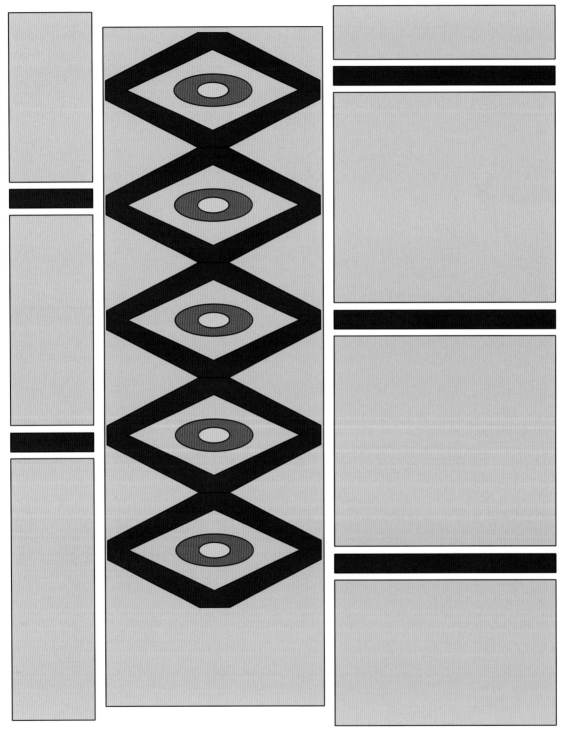

Final quilt assembly

Quilting diagram

**Enlarge patterns
400%**

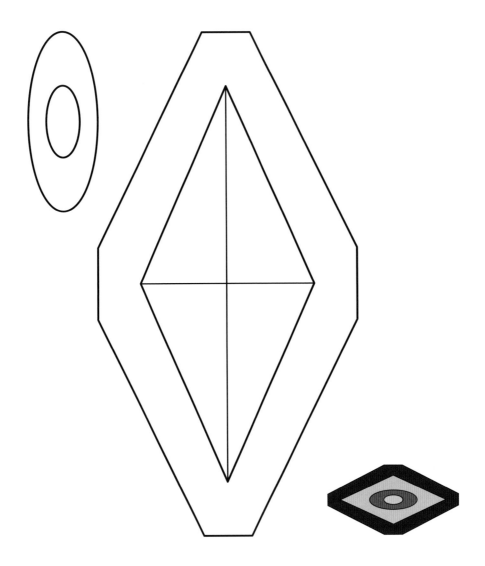

SLICE IT UP, 52" x 72". Designed and pieced by Nancy Gano.
Quilted by Janice Kiser of the Ewe Tree.

··· SLICE IT UP ···

52" x 72"

Fabric Requirements

White – 4¼ yards *(background and binding)*

Coral – ¼ yard

Blue – Three (3) assorted shades, ½ yard
each shade *(appliqué shapes)*

Backing – 3½ yards

Fusible web or appliqué interfacing for
your chosen appliqué method

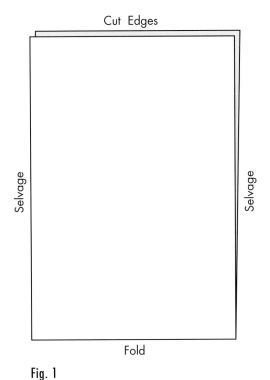

Cut Edges

Selvage

Selvage

Fold

Fig. 1

Cutting

White

Cut two (2) 16½" x WOF strips
Subcut two (2) 16½" x 36½" rectangles

> **NOTE:** You will be cutting the remaining
> pieces LOF (length of fabric), NOT
> WOF. Before cutting, fold the remaining
> fabric with the cut edges together, and
> selvage edges on both sides, fig. 1.

Cut one (1) 33½" x LOF strip,
Subcut one (1) 33½" x 72½" rectangle

Cut three (3) 2¼" x LOF strips (binding)

Coral

Cut two (2) 3½" x WOF strips
Subcut two (2) 3½" x 36½" strips

Blue

Using the 8" full circle template on p. 77,
cut three (3). One (1) of each shade.

Using the 8" half circle template on the
same page, cut seven (7) two (2) of
each shade and one (1) additional of
Dark shade.

Assembly

Using the appliqué shapes, p. 77, and your favorite appliqué method, create the appliqué units on the White background. Refer to the final quilt assembly diagram, p. 75, for appliqué placement.

Refer to the quilt assemblely diagram, p. 74, to piece the three (3) individual units together.

TIP

Fold White sections in half lengthwise, right sides together and lightly press the fold using an iron. This crease will help serve as your guideline to attach the appliqué shapes.

Quilt as desired, or as shown in the provided quilting diagram, p. 76. Bind using the provided instructions on pp. 16–17 (Finishing the Quilt) or your favorite binding method.

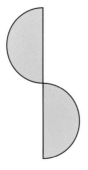

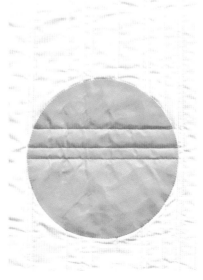

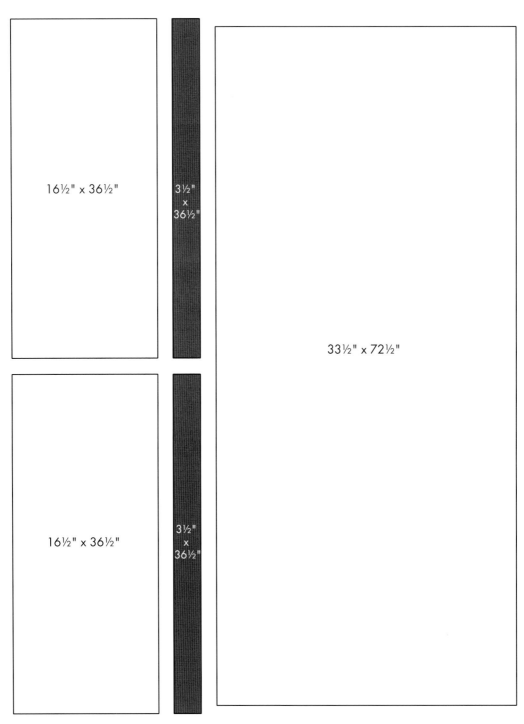

16½" x 36½"   3½"
              x
              36½"

33½" x 72½"

16½" x 36½"   3½"
              x
              36½"

Quilt assembly

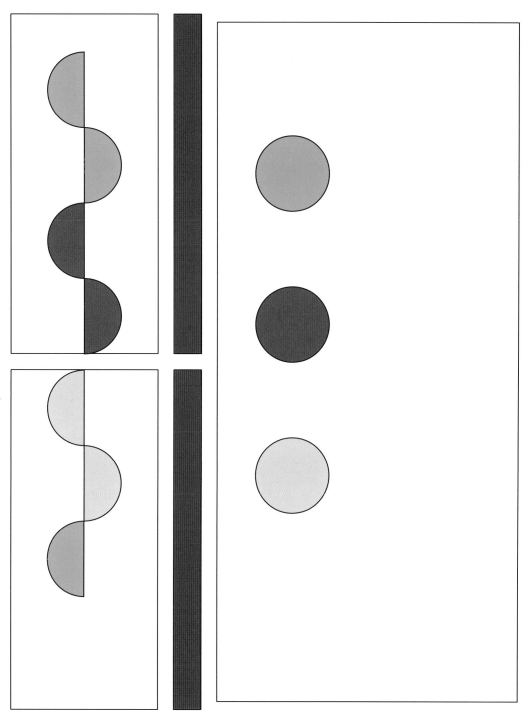

Final quilt assembly

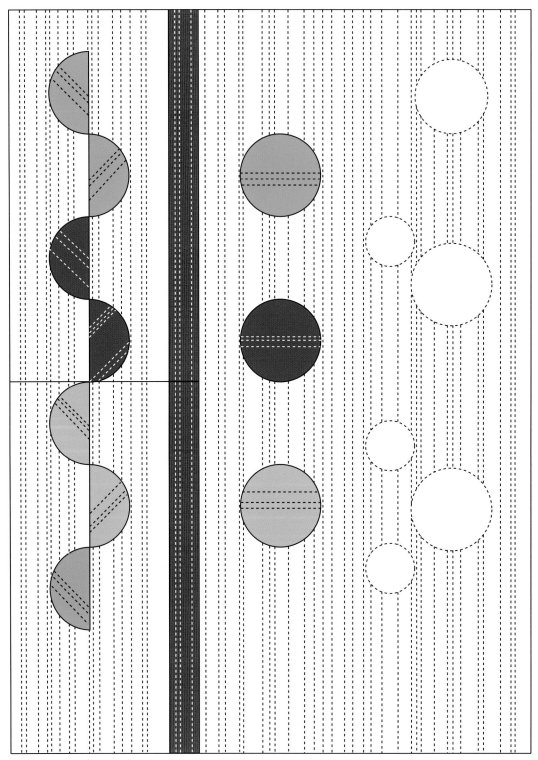

Quilting diagram

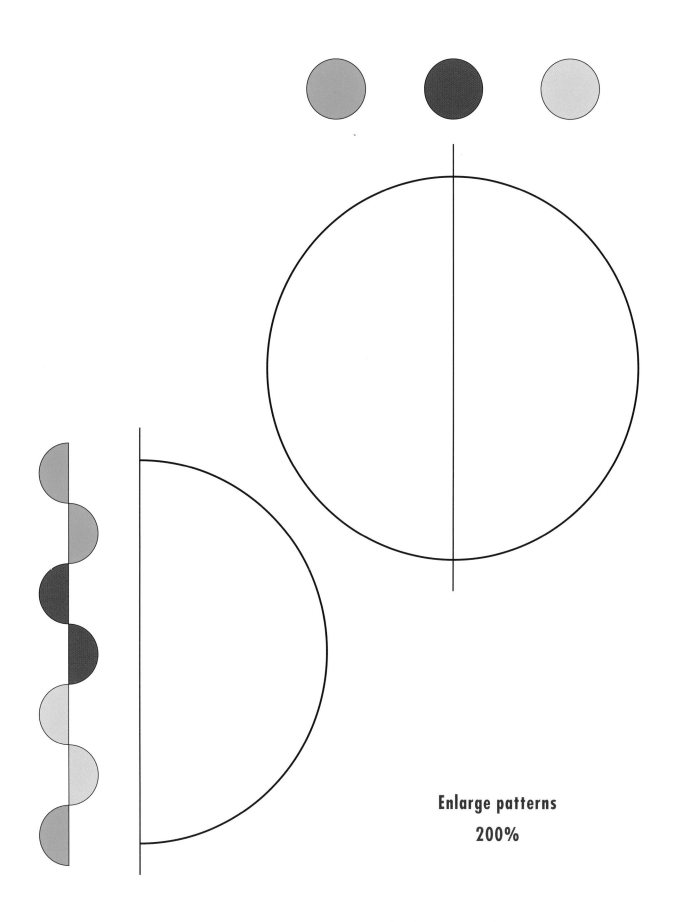

**Enlarge patterns
200%**

URBAN GARDEN, 62" x 80". Designed, pieced, and quilted by Nancy Gano

Appliqué for MODERN Beginners ✦ *Eva Birch, Nancy Gano, & Jodi Robinson*

Urban Garden

62" x 80"

Fabric Requirements

Brown – 1½ yards *(appliqué background)*
Green – 3 assorted shades, ½ yard each
  shade *(appliqué shapes)*
Cream – 4 yards *(background and binding)*
Backing – 4 yards
Fusible web or appliqué interfacing for
  your chosen appliqué method

Cutting

Brown

Cut four (4) 8½" x WOF strips
  Subcut one (1) 8½" x 8½" square
    One (1) 8½" x 12½" rectangle
    One (1) 8½" x 14½" rectangle
    One (1) 8½" x 16½" rectangle
    One (1) 8½" x 24½" rectangle
    One (1) 8½" x 28½" rectangle
    One (1) 8½" x 34½" rectangle

Assorted Greens (3)

Cut (2) 4½" x WOF strips of each color
  Subcut **Light Green**:
    One (1) 4½" x 12½" – Unit C
    One (1) 4½" x 16½" – Unit A
    One (1) 4½" x 28½" – Unit B

  Subcut **Medium Green**
    One (1) 4½" x 18½" – Unit F
    One (1) 4½" x 38½" – Unit G

  Subcut **Dark Green**
    One (1) 4½" x 20½" – Unit E
    One (1) 4½" x 32½" – Unit D

Cream

Cut five (5) 6½" x WOF strips
 Subcut one (1) 6½" x 25½" rectangle
  One (1) 6½" x 36½" rectangle
  One (1) 6½" x 19½" rectangle
  One (1) 6½" x 43½" rectangle
  One (1) 6½" x 37½" rectangle

Cut three (3) 8½" x WOF strips
 Subcut three (3) 8½" x 4½" rectangle
  Two (2) 8½" x 5½" rectangle
  One (1) 8½" x 6½" rectangle
  Two (2) 8½" x 7½" rectangle
  Two (2) 8½" x 8½" squares
  Two (2) 8½" x 9½" rectangle
  One (1) 8½" x 12½" rectangle
  One (1) 8½" x 16½" rectangle

Cut two (2) 12½" x WOF, sew ends together
 Subcut one (1) 12½" x 34½" rectangle
  One (1) 12½" x 46½" rectangle

Cut two (2) 14½" x WOF, sew ends together
 Subcut one (1) 14½" x 34½" rectangle
  One (1) 14½" x 46½" rectangle

Cut eight (8) 2¼" x WOF strips (binding)

Assembly

Referring to the quilt assembly diagram, p. 81, sew Cream and Brown pieces to create background units A – G.

Using the assorted Green strips, create your appliqué shapes by using template on p. 84. The template is to be used to round the corners of the strips. Align the template so the curved edge is at end of the strip. Trace the template and cut the corners out.

With your prepared appliqué shapes and your chosen appliqué method, center shapes over the background units A – G as shown in the final quilt assembly diagram, p 82. Appliqué in place.

Sew the two (2) remaining Cream pieces to the right sides of Units F and G as shown in the quilt assembly diagram.

Sew all units together according to the quilt assembly diagram.

Quilt as desired, or as shown in the provided quilting diagram, p. 83. Bind using the provided instructions on pp. 16–17 (Finishing the Quilt) or your favorite binding method.

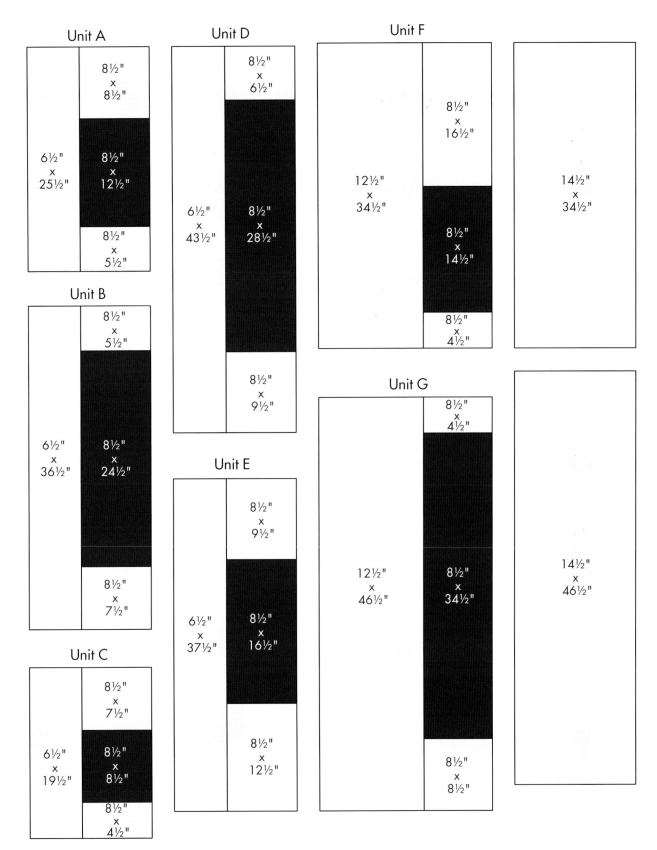

Unit A

8½"
x
8½"

6½"
x
25½"

8½"
x
12½"

8½"
x
5½"

Unit B

8½"
x
5½"

6½"
x
36½"

8½"
x
24½"

8½"
x
7½"

Unit C

8½"
x
7½"

6½"
x
19½"

8½"
x
8½"

8½"
x
4½"

Unit D

8½"
x
6½"

6½"
x
43½"

8½"
x
28½"

8½"
x
9½"

Unit E

8½"
x
9½"

6½"
x
37½"

8½"
x
16½"

8½"
x
12½"

Unit F

8½"
x
16½"

12½"
x
34½"

8½"
x
14½"

8½"
x
4½"

14½"
x
34½"

Unit G

8½"
x
4½"

12½"
x
46½"

8½"
x
34½"

8½"
x
8½"

14½"
x
46½"

Quilt assembly

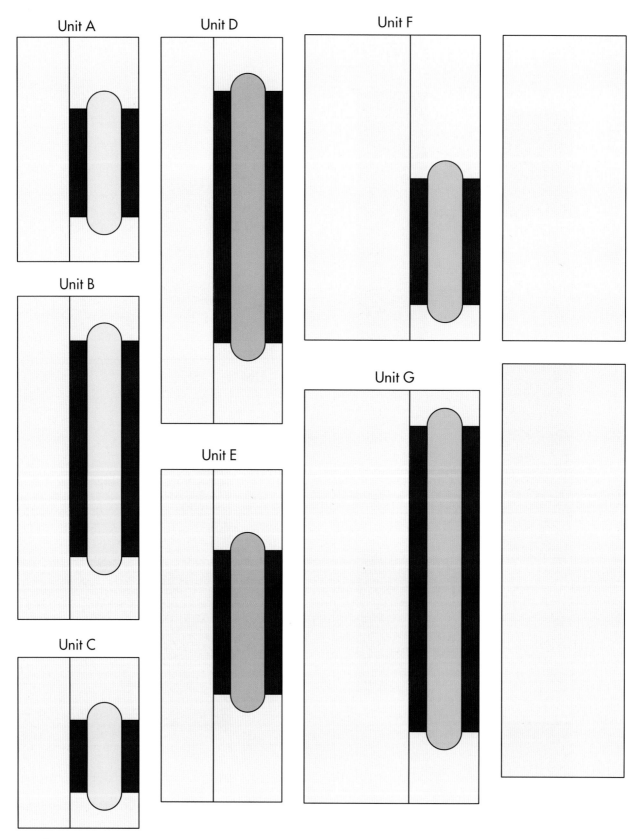

Unit A

Unit B

Unit C

Unit D

Unit E

Unit F

Unit G

Final quilt assembly

Quilting diagram. *Woodgrain*, pantograph pattern, designed by Lisa Thiessen, Willow Leaf Studio, 2005.

Pattern shown

100%

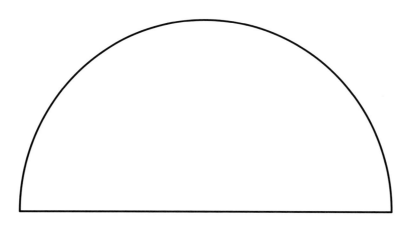

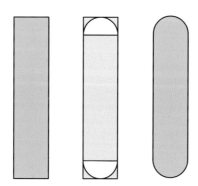

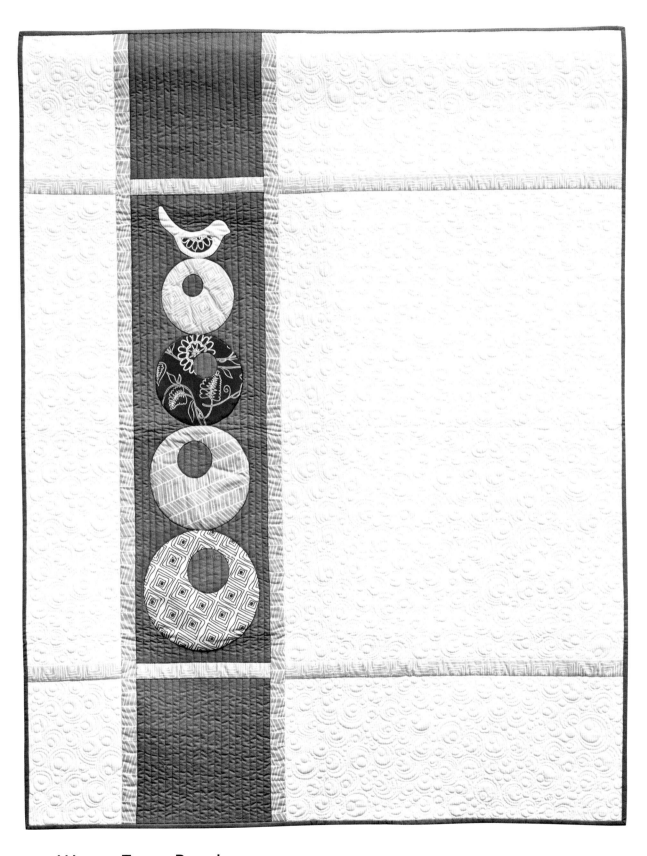

WHAT A TWEET BABY!, 40" x 50". Designed, pieced, and quilted by Jodi Robinson

... WHAT A TWEET BABY! ...

40" X 50"

Fabric Requirements

Gray – 1 yard *(appliqué background and binding, appliqué bird)*

White – 1½ Yards

Turquoise print – ¼ yard *(sashing strips)*

Turquoise and coral prints – scraps *(appliqué circles and bird wing)*

Backing – 1¾ yards

Fusible web or appliqué interfacing for your chosen appliqué method

Cutting
Gray

Cut five (5) 2¼" x WOF strips (binding)

Cut one (1) 9½" x 30½" rectangle (appliqué background)

Cut two (2) 9½" x 9½" squares

White

Cut one (1) 6½" x 30½" strip

Cut one (1) 23½" x 30½" rectangle

Cut two (2) 9½" x WOF strips
    Subcut one (2) 6½" x 9½" rectangle
        Two (2) 23½" x 9½" rectangle

Turquoise

Cut five (5) 1½" x WOF strips
    From two (2) of the 1½" strips,
    Subcut two (2) 6½" x 1½" strips
        Two (2) 9½" x 1½" strips
        Two (2) 23½" x 1½" strips

Appliqué for MODERN Beginners ✦ *Eva Birch, Nancy Gano, & Jodi Robinson*

Assembly

Using the appliqué template shapes, p. 91, and your favorite appliqué method, create the appliqué panel on the 9½" x 30½" Gray appliqué background. Refer to the final quilt assembly diagram, p. 89, for appliqué placement.

Refer to the quilt assembly diagram, p. 88, to piece the three (3) individual quilt sections.

NOTE: For the center quilt section, you will need to join (3) Turquoise 1½" x WOF strips end to end, to create one continuous strip. This strip will be more than long enough for both sides of this section.

Join the three (3) individual sections to complete the quilt top

Quilt as desired, or as shown in the provided quilting diagram, p. 90. Bind using the provided instructions on pp. 16–17 (Finishing the Quilt) or your favorite binding method.

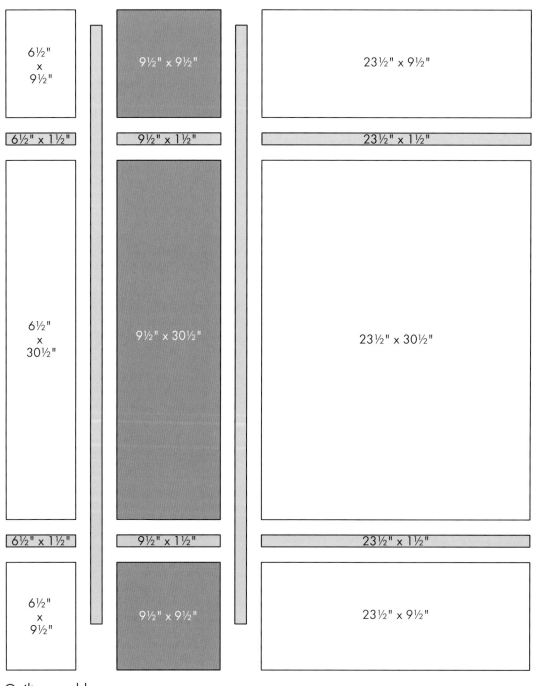

6½"
x
9½"

9½" x 9½"

23½" x 9½"

6½" x 1½"

9½" x 1½"

23½" x 1½"

6½"
x
30½"

9½" x 30½"

23½" x 30½"

6½" x 1½"

9½" x 1½"

23½" x 1½"

6½"
x
9½"

9½" x 9½"

23½" x 9½"

Quilt assembly

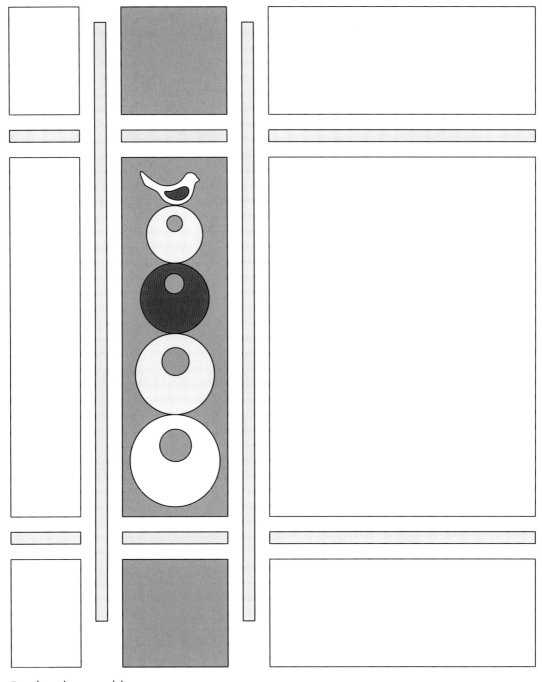

Final quilt assembly

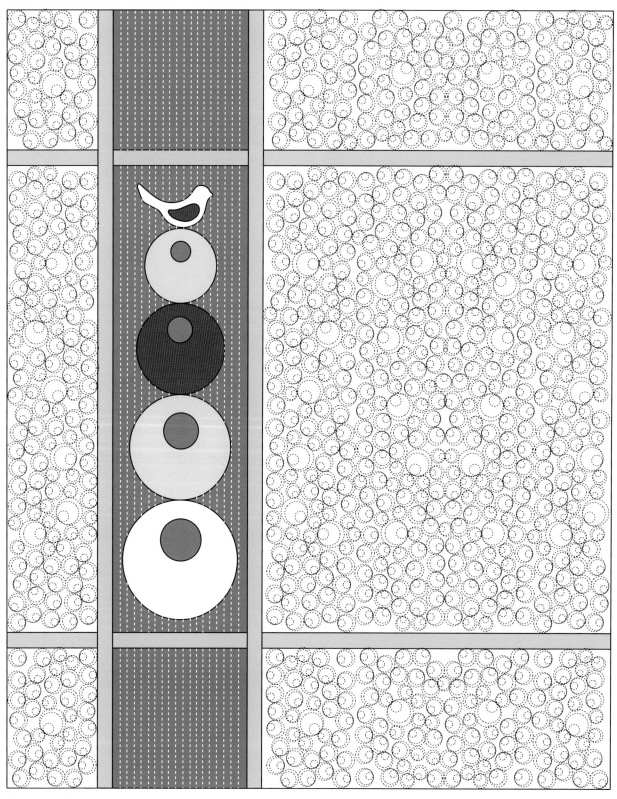

Quilting diagram

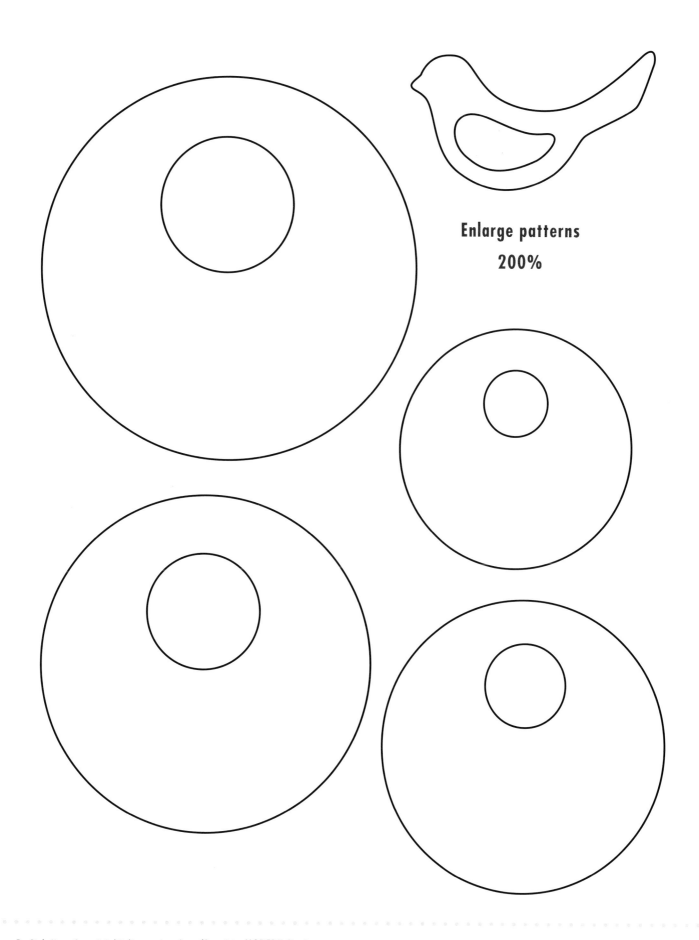

Enlarge patterns

200%

References and Resources

References

Piece by Piece Machine Appliqué
Sharon Shamber and Cristy Fincher
Paducah, KY, American Quilters Society, 2007

Resources

Sharon's Secret Foundation
Water soluble foundation paper
sharonshamber.com
purpledaisiesquilting.com

Ricky Tim's Stable Stuff Poly
Versatile multi-purpose stabilizer
rickytims.com

C&T Publishing Wash Away Appliqué Roll
Fusible water soluble foundation paper

Pellon®
Pellon 805 Wonder-Under® Paper-Backed
Transfer Web
pelloninterlinings.com

Superior Threads™
Monopoly
Superiorthreads.com

Gammill®
For making an amazing Longarm machine that allows us to be creative and turn our dreams into reality.
Gammill.net

... About the Authors ...

We wanted to share our thoughts on the creation of this book. It was our passion to create and our Gammill longarm quilting machines that brought us together several years ago, when we met at our longarm quilting guild, the Ohio Longarm Quilters. Although our designing, piecing, and quilting talents vary, we all thoroughly enjoy the overall process of creating, and seeing our visions come to life. We are thankful for the friendships developed over the years. Who better to offer advice on color selections, sizing proportions, and thread choices than our more knowledgeable friends? We've thought about this adventure for some time, and with the modern quilt movement on the rise, the timing was perfect. Our hope is that we inspire you to create some graphic, modern quilts of your own. Get creative, get bold, and have fun exploring appliqué. As you will learn, the possibilities are endless!

Eva Birch

PHOTO: Photo Innovations

Eva has been a quilter for nine years, and a professional Longarm Quilter for eight years. She has been teaching both locally and nationally for the past two years. Eva has won several national awards for her own and customer quilts. Eva's work has been published in several quilting publications. She enjoys quilting with a passion, and loves to share her creativity with her students, and other quilters. Her machine quilting business, Stitch by Stitch Creations, is located in Mantua, Ohio. Aside from quilting, Eva enjoys spending time with her husband, children, and grandchildren.

Nancy Gano

PHOTO: Sketch Studio

Nancy has been a quilter for the past 25 years, and has been a professional Longarm Machine Quilter for 12 years. She is an award winning quilter, and has been teaching on the local level for the past several years. Nancy's quilts have been published in several quilting publications. Her real love in the quilting process lies in the design and piecing.

Jodi Robinson

PHOTO: Bonnie McCaffery Photography

Jodi has been a quilter for well over 20 years, and a professional Longarm Quilter for the past 19 years. She has been teaching nationally for the past 11 years. She has won numerous national awards for her quilts and machine quilting skills. Most recently, she won Best Modern Quilt awards at some of the AQS shows in 2014, and the Outstanding Modern Quilt award in 2015. In addition to teaching, she designs digitized machine quilting designs, and has self-published nine machine quilting design books. Jodi is a Gammill Quilting Artist, and operates a machine quilting business in Enon Valley, PA called JR Designs, providing longarm machine quilting services to her clients. Visit her blog to see what she is working on: http://jrdesigns.wordpress.com.

#102772

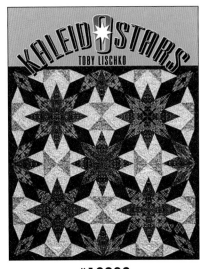

#10283

#10310

Enjoy these and more from AQS

AQS Publishing brings the latest in quilt topics to satisfy the traditional to modern quilter. Interesting techniques, vivid color, and clear directions make these books your one-stop for quilt design and instruction. With its leading Quilt-Fiction series, mystery, relationship, and community all merge as stories are pieced together to keep you spell-bound.

Whether Quilt-Instruction or Quilt-Fiction, pick one up from AQS today.

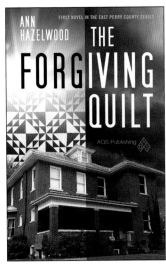

#10279

#10286

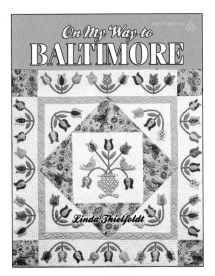

#10308

AQS publications are available nationwide.
Call or visit AQS
www.shopAQS.com
1-800-626-5420